SAVAGE OXYGEN

BY CHRISTOPHER SAVAGE

ABOUT CHRIS SAVAGE

Chris Savage inspires growth in leaders, teams and businesses around the world. He is one of Asia Pacific's pre-eminent communications, public relations and professional services industry leaders. Chris is also an internationally renowned motivational speaker on personal, professional and business growth. His weekly blog, *Wrestling Possums* (www.chrisjohnsavage.com), is widely read globally. His passion is learning, and to share experiences with others keen for growth. Chris lives in Sydney, Australia.

Dedication

With appreciation and love to the source of my joy: Sophia, Antonia, Ben and Katrina.

Savage Oxygen is self-published by Chris Savage via createspace.com and is a work of non-fiction.

Published in 2016.
Available in the Kindle store and from worldwide Amazon sites.

HOW TO READ

Any way you like! It can be read from start to finish. Or dip in and out, sampling stories at random.

The book has three sections:

Section One   If You're Green, You Grow
Section Two   Leadership Lessons from the Front Line
Section Three Habits to Help You Thrive

Within each section are individual stories, designed to elaborate on themes and chapter headings. There is some repetition of ideas. This is to make sure those 'dipping in randomly' don't miss out on important messages.

However you go about it, *Savage Oxygen* WILL make a difference to you. Breathe in the inspiration from these stories. They will give you heart just when you need it. Promise!

SECTION ONE: IF YOU'RE GREEN, YOU GROW

SECTION TWO: LEADERSHIP LESSONS FROM THE FRONT LINE

TAKE ACTION

SET ACHIEVABLE, SHORT-TERM GOALS

FACE REALITY

SHARPEN YOUR JUDGMENT

SET THE EXAMPLE

KNOW WHEN TO SHOW UP

BE PARANOID

EMBRACE CHANGE

BE RELENTLESSLY PERSISTENT

PLAY WHAT IS IN FRONT OF YOU

INSPIRE, INSPIRE, INSPIRE

STOP BEING SO BLOODY BUSY

SECTION THREE: HABITS TO HELP YOU THRIVE

LEVERAGE YOUR SPECIAL TALENTS

STAY CONNECTED, PASSIONATELY

BE OPTIMISTIC

YOU ARE YOUR SCHEDULE

NURTURE RELATIONSHIPS

TAKE DELIBERATE OXYGEN

GRATEFULNESS/JOY

SENSE OF PURPOSE

UNDERSTAND YOURSELF

PUT PRESSURE ON YOURSELF

BE YOUR OWN BEST COACH

TAKE RESPONSIBILITY

FINAL POSTSCRIPT

ACKNOWLEDGMENTS & THANKS

REFERENCES & SOURCES

SAVAGE OXYGEN

INTRODUCTION

All my career I had been the youngest person in the room: the bright, high-potential executive rapidly climbing the ladder. One day I paused to look around me and, to my great surprise, I realised that I had become – at 50 years old – the oldest person in the room.

How is it, I asked myself, that I have survived in my career, am thriving, and have many exciting opportunities winking at me beyond my current role? How is it that, in my little world, I am still wanted, relevant and able to add value? How is it that I am still engaged with brilliantly talented young people, learning more than ever before and still presented with exciting challenges to throw myself at?

What happened to everyone else? Where are those colleagues who were with me along the way? How is it I ended up the oldest person in the room?

I came to realise Vidal Sassoon showed me the way, when he told me 20 years ago: *'The only place where success comes before work is in the dictionary.'*

From that day I became determined to work on myself as a project for the rest of my career: to work on myself even harder than I worked on my job. *Savage Oxygen* shares lessons from that journey: as a leader of teams, businesses, clients and in leading my greatest ally and enemy – myself.

These experiences helped me deal with my constant fear, negative thoughts, low self-esteem, fragile self-respect and the shame I felt in just being me. I managed (and manage) to cover it up with bravado – by putting on a performance of strength and confidence, boldness and fortitude. Behind the facade, there was deep doubt, loneliness, substance abuse, comfort binge eating and lots of counselling. Thankfully, I have been blessed with love and support all along the way of my little journey.

Many of the stories in this book first appeared on my blog, *Wrestling Possums*. I was inspired to start the blog for two reasons.

First, as an example to leaders in my business, whom I wanted to encourage to build their company and personal brands through social media. Many of my early posts focused on professional services, and how to deliver better customer service.

With time, my second motivation became clearer. There were many 'life lessons' I wanted to share with my children. If I lived long enough, I would tell them these stories myself. But if I died now, I wanted to have them written down. At some point they might read them, and get value and guidance from my experiences.

I believe our legacies are what we teach. As the Greek statesman Pericles said: *'What you leave behind is not what is engraved in stone monuments, but what is woven into the lives of others'*. I wanted to be able to weave into the lives of my children the very best life lessons I have learnt. As Sydney business leader Geoff Levy told me: *'You can take the learning without having to go through the lessons yourself'*.

As the texture of my content evolved, reader feedback became more heartfelt, personal and profound. I was clearly striking a chord. So I have continued telling stories from the heart, often exposing vulnerabilities and weaknesses.

Not everyone liked this approach. Feedback in a work appraisal a couple of years ago criticised: *'Don't show vulnerability in your blog. Never show weakness. We must be seen as strong, always'*. What rubbish! It is only when we are vulnerable that we truly connect with people in ways that matter.

A final thought before you begin. Leonard Cohen wrote in 'Going Home':

'He will speak these words of wisdom
Like a sage, a man of vision
Though he knows he's really nothing
But the brief elaboration of a tune ...'

That's me. No man of vision. No sage. Just a brief elaboration of a story, an experience – sometimes an insight – that was meaningful to me as I battled on in my career and life. And as I continue to do so today. Granted – usually pretty glib, light on, trite, often 'bus ticket' material. Given that my target market for this book includes those beginning careers, I'm heartened by the old adage, *'Every joke is new to an 11-year-old'*. Clichés perhaps, but nonetheless vital messages for those in their salad days. Perhaps there is something in these pages for you? I hope so. There has been for me.

If I had a magic wand, I'd use it to make sure as many 18-year-olds as possible had a copy of *Savage Oxygen* on their bedside tables, or Kindles. It's relevant to all ages. I just wish I had known some of this stuff 30 years ago. It would have been my *vade mecum,* a guide that is kept constantly at hand for consultation.

Wrestling Possums cleanses me a little. It helps me be the real me. And again with thanks to Leonard, now that *Savage Oxygen* is done, I can feel like I am: *'Going home without my burden ... Going home without the costume that I wore'.*

I hope you enjoy. If you do, tell everyone! If you don't, tell me!

Chris Savage

From a 'Third Place' somewhere.

WHY 'WRESTLING POSSUMS'?

A possum climbed through my window late one night. It saw a naked me and was petrified (fair enough). I chased it around the room, finally pouncing on it with a towel. It was immediately still. I let it loose outside. It shot away and was gone. We are similar. Adventurous yet easily frightened. Occasionally compliant but normally happiest left alone to do it our own way.

Plus 'possum' is the affectionate Australian vernacular for someone we care for, made famous by Dame Edna Everage. To grow relationships, businesses, potential, effectiveness, meaning and happiness, we have to wrestle, possums!

SECTION ONE
IF YOU'RE GREEN, YOU GROW

Are you ripe? If so, watch out! You will rot, and drop off the tree. Rather, be green. Stay eager to learn, improve, evolve and grow. Sample the stories in this introductory section for ideas on how to approach working on yourself, and to embrace improvement and a 'growth mindset'. You never know: it might just inspire you to action!

1.1
VIDAL SASSOON TOLD ME THIS KEY TO SUCCESS

To hairdressers, Vidal Sassoon is still a rock star. It was something he told me 20 years ago that I want to share. It startled me when he said it, and the truth resounds just as powerfully today. Here's the story.

Vidal Sassoon – self-made, highly driven and from a grindingly poor background – revolutionised the hairdressing craft. His obituary in *The Sydney Morning Herald* read: *'An astute businessman, he made a fortune from his salons and products, and became a household name'.*

While at lunch with him during a promotional tour we coordinated in the mid-1990s, I asked him about his success and fame. What he told me has ever since underpinned my approach to my career and life, and is something I have shared with as many people as I can.

'You know, when I die I will probably be remembered most not for what I achieved in the hairdressing industry – but rather for something I once said. You'll find this attributed to me in most books of quotes.'

The only place where success comes before work is in a dictionary.

Think about it. If you want to succeed (however you define success), you have to work at it. Consistently. Persistently. I am a great believer in this philosophy. Here's why.

During the first 20 years of my career, my star rose faster than others because I quite simply worked harder than anyone else. I certainly was not smarter, so I drove my career through bloody hard work. Consistently. Persistently.

Now, maybe I went too far. For many years I devoted my life, literally, to work. I'd work most weekends, and long hours during the week. Regrets? A few. In truth, I loved it.

I do shake my head in wonder at young people coming into business, expecting fame and fortune without being prepared to put in the effort. Some will be horrified by such an 'old-fashioned' view. So be it. Fact is, I have never seen anyone 'succeed' (in anything) without working really, really hard at it. Sometimes, frankly, that involves long hours, and certainly so in the early years.

I've had feedback from many who disagree – they feel efficiency and effectiveness is the key, not 'time at work'. I agree. For me it's about both – being highly efficient, focusing on key priorities AND, working harder than the rest.

Remember *'there are no crowds lining the extra mile'*. We're alone – just us and the challenge we've set ourselves. The reality is this: *'Champions do extra'*. It's as simple as that. If you want to succeed, you need to choose to make the effort and sacrifice it takes to get there.

I remain a consistent, persistent hard worker today. I have worked hard to be as productive and efficient as I can be – to ensure I get more of the important things done every day. In this way, I have more time for the rest of my life.

If you want to 'succeed' and achieve your potential, you have to be prepared to put in the hard yards when it counts. Those 'yards' are always about how seriously you are taking yourself, and your progress. You have to work on yourself – like a project.

Remember, the only place **success** comes before **work** is in a dictionary. It's not always about long hours (though sometimes it simply is). It's about working on it. Working on it. Working on it. Enough already. I have to get back to work.

1.2
EAT THIS AND YOU WILL BE A TRUE CHAMPION

In Andre Agassi's fridge lies the answer to the type of diet we need to feast on if we want to be the best we can be. I find it hard to swallow. Do you?

A friend once asked the guy next to him on a plane what he did for a living. *'I'm one of tennis player Andre Agassi's three backhand coaches,'* the man apparently replied.

WOW! Three backhand coaches! Agassi was clearly a guy who relished feedback. The lesson is clear. We need to become feedback gluttons if we are to reach our full potential. Agassi epitomised a key habit of winners.

Feedback is the food of champions.

Now, I love feedback, so long as it's positive. If it's not, then I spiral into a series of emotions: from outright rejection, to anger, depression, resentfulness and, finally, to vengefulness. I get damned determined to fix the issue so the person who gave me the feedback can never say that about me again! This ultimately leads to proactive action, to my embracing the feedback and doing something about it. And then being grateful for it. It's a struggle.

I wish I'd been more proactive and persistent in seeking feedback during my career. I would have grown, learnt and achieved more. And made more friends along the way.

My problem, until a few years ago, was that I was stuck in a fixed mindset. I naively believed I had reached the peak of my abilities and had little to learn. So I felt I had to prove myself over and over again, and vigorously resist any suggestions I was not perfect.

Stop! Instead, cultivate a *growth* mindset, based on the belief that your basic qualities are things you can cultivate through your efforts. Thrive on setbacks and feedback as a springboard for growth and stretching your existing abilities. I read this 'growth' mindset creates a passion for learning rather than a hunger for approval.

So, don't make my mistake. Please. Become feedback junkies. Don't look for praise. Look for honest, 'warts and all' feedback. It really is the food of champions. And it's not easy to do. For me, anyway.

Postscript

I was in a cinema in the New South Wales coastal town of Ulladulla, bored to distraction watching the Dr Seuss movie, *The Lorax*. The Lorax is the 'protector of the trees'. During the film, the Lorax said something that jolted me to full attention. It was a message that changed my path forever.

The Lorax is talking to his adversary, who wants to destroy the forest: '*Hey*,' he asks, '*which way do trees fall?*' '*I don't know*,' was the reply from his antagonist. '*Which way do trees fall?*' '*They fall the way they lean. Watch out which way you lean.*'

Which way are you leaning right now in your career, life, key relationships and health? Are you leaning towards complacency? Watch out. That's the way you will fall.

Or are you leaning towards giving yourself feedback, growing, not resting on your laurels, making the effort to work on yourself like a project?

Remember, you **will** fall the way you are leaning. Take action now to lean the right way. Please.

1.3
THE CHARGING BLACK RHINO AND WOODY ALLEN

The black rhino was 20 metres away, angry, travelling fast, horn lowered for action, and charging right at me. Did my life flash before me? No. All I could think about was Woody Allen. Here's why.

Before dawn, and in the late afternoons, we'd go out into the reserve in an open-air jeep searching for game. We saw amazing things. Leopards up a tree protecting a kill (impala), with four lions trying to climb it. Lions mating. Leopards fighting with hyenas. Hippos. Elephants. The works. It was exhilarating, and exhausting. Our last dawn arrived. It was 5am, dark and freezing. We'd already done five long drives over two and a half days. Should we get up for one more game drive? Or had we had enough?

'Let's do it!' we agreed, and so fate brought us to Woody Allen, who once expressed this most profound truth:

85% of the secret of success is just turning up.

As that black rhino charged, I felt no fear. Just surprise. *'Crikey,'* I mused. *'I did not expect this to happen. How interesting!'* Then I thought of Woody. Yip – I'd 'turned up' and pushed myself just that extra step. No warm bed and coffee. Instead, bracing cold darkness, a bouncing jeep and the likelihood of seeing nothing new. Now here was a massive and grumpy beast rumbling towards me. How amazing!

Our ranger revved the jeep engine loudly, and he and the tracker yelled obscenities at the rhino. No kidding. At the last moment, it skidded to a halt. Shaking its head violently, and after glaring at me with some menace, it did a 360 and calmly trotted away. It was about two metres away when it stopped its charge.

'Just turning up.' Yes, it can mean physically 'turning up'. But it's more about pushing yourself to take the initiative, to go that extra step. To make the effort.

I 'turned up' in Adelaide in 1979, the day I landed in Australia, by walking into a pancake restaurant and asking for a job. I started that night and stayed five years while doing my university degree. I 'turned up' in 1992 when I proactively rang a Lend Lease shopping centre manager to offer help on a small PR issue. During the next 20 years my agencies earned $20 million in fees from Lend Lease (and we made lifelong friends, too). I 'turned up' when I decided three years ago to 'get online' to really understand how social media worked. That's when I started my blog – now with 11,000 weekly subscribers and followers. I started by writing 13 weeks' worth of *Possums* posts on a flight from Sydney to Shanghai. That gave me the momentum to get the thing going. I 'turned up' on that flight for me. I could easily have watched five movies.

'Turning up' is about not taking the easy route. It's about pushing yourself. Make that call, attend the breakfast speech, read a book on the plane, make contact with that person, have the courage to ask for feedback. Dip in to *Savage Oxygen* daily and take a message from it of value to you. Push yourself into action.

I got charged by a black rhino. I am going to remember that a lot longer than two extra hours of sleep and a coffee in bed. Remember – 85% of the secret of success IS just turning up. It really is.

Postscript One

I was giving a speech at a conference in Johannesburg. I rehearsed during the tea break once the hundreds of attendees had left the auditorium for morning tea. One of my slides was a picture of Woody Allen, with the 'turning up' message. There was one guy sitting in the otherwise empty auditorium watching me. As I finished rehearsing, he bounded up to me. Heavy South African accent. *'I love that Woody slide,'* he said. *'I couldn't agree more. I was telling my "Lighty" that message just the other day ... That "just turning up" is a secret to success.'* (Lighty is slang for younger person or son). I paid scant attention, thanked him a little irritably, made my speech a few minutes later, and then sat down to watch the next speaker. Hang on. It's the bloke who came up to me in the break – the guy who told me he is a true believer that 'just turning up' is a secret to success. Who is he? Aaah, it's Robbie Brozin, cofounder of the global Nando's chicken chain. Point made.

Postscript Two

I hate shopping. Some time ago, I needed work shoes, but despite being in the city, I couldn't find any I liked. Extremely grumpily, I walked into Bally. I'd never been in there before. I looked at their shoes. Expensive!!! Triple what I'd normally pay. I was readying to leave when a young shop assistant approached. *'So, what Bally shoes are you wearing?'* I growled at him. *'Well, sir,'* he replied, *'I am on probation – just been here a week. They give me this pair during this period. If I pass muster and they keep me, then I get that pair.'* He pointed to a shiny work shoe. I picked it up. Tried it on. It was expensive. *'No, it's not for me,'* I replied. *'Why not?'* he asked. *'Well, you see how it has a ridge, or strip, across the width of the shoe. I don't like that strip.'* I was getting ruder and gruffer. I expected him to retreat and just leave me alone. *'Sir,'* he replied, *'may I just have a moment to point something out? You see, that strip is vital to keeping the shoe looking new for longer. Without it, the shoe will quickly crease, and age. But with it, that shoe will look new and sharp in two years' time.'*

I paused. Hmmm. That made sense. I liked that. I wanted shoes with that strip. I looked up at him. *'Young shaver – I'll take them.'* I went downstairs. *'Are you the manager?'* I asked a managerial looking person. 'Yes,' she replied. *'Well, hire that young guy upstairs immediately. He just "turned up" for you. He went the extra step, and pushed himself to take a risk, persist with a grumpy and intimidating customer, and sold me a $700 pair of shoes.'*

So it came to pass. He was hired the next day. Works there now (as a manager), and reads *Possums* weekly. He is still 'turning up'. It's a secret of success.

1.4
WHY I TOLD THE MONK NOT TO F**K WITH MICKEY

Monks are gentle, peace-loving people. So why was I paralysed with fear when I looked one particular monk in the eyes and said: *'OK – I will start very slowly. But beware. Whatever you do, don't f**k with Mickey?'* Here's why.

A Walt Disney CEO, who when advised by a consultant to refresh the Disney logo, apparently said, very bluntly: *'Don't f**k with Mickey'*. The Mickey logo was sacrosanct: a proven, well-loved symbol of everything the company stood for. It was never to be tampered with.

That was equally true with what the monk wanted to do to me that day. I just wasn't having any of it.

You see, he wanted to help me learn and grow … to help me change and evolve.

Outrageous! *'Look,'* I said to him, *'what I do and the way I am is a proven package, developed and fine-tuned over a long career. It works. It has given me professional success and helped me achieve many goals. So while I am kind of okay to have you teach me new stuff, I'll only do it if you don't tamper with the proven package that is the "Chris at work" me. Don't f**k with Mickey.'*

The monk (well, he used to be a monk; now he's an inspiring leadership coach and teacher) replied: *'Chris, you sound like Winston Churchill, who said something like: "I am keen to learn, but am a very reluctant student!"'* He was right! I was petrified that somehow I'd change and be less effective.

Doug Smollan, the chairman of field marketing leader Smollan Group, gave me the confidence to embrace learning again. Doug's mantra is this:

If you're green, you grow; if you're ripe, you rot.

People who are content with who they are and what they bring are often arrogant. *'Arrogance and ego is the start of ripeness and the beginning of the rot,'* Doug says. *'Stay green – physically, mentally, spiritually and in your relationships.'*

You can't help others reach their highest potential unless you're in the process of reaching for yours. Lead yourself first. Work harder on yourself than you do on your job.

Be addicted to learning. I spent 20 years in the darkness of arrogance and ego, thinking I knew it all. I didn't. I don't. My Mickey needs continual redesigning and refreshing. Doug opened my eyes. I have confronted my fears, and now – as I move deeper into my 50s – I am passionate about learning new stuff. And for sharing what I know to help others (who want it) to grow. It inspires and energises me. And I am having the time of my life!

Remember – if you're green, you grow; if you're ripe, you rot.

And your Mickey will thank you for regular tampering. That is for sure. Give it a go!

1.5
COMING SECOND WILL HELP ENSURE YOU WIN – EVERY TIME

I have always believed that to succeed, 'being first' would be a bloody good place to start. I was wrong. The fact is, coming second, or even third, is critical to succeeding in business and in life.

Malcolm Gladwell speaks about how innovators are often not the ones who end up commercialising their innovations. Rather, someone else sees, tweaks, refines, popularises, and makes a fortune out of it.

I liked the concept, but did not really understand the point, until I read this from Australian rugby union legend and now leadership coach, John Eales:

The early bird gets the worm, but the second mouse gets the cheese.

That's it! The second mouse gets the cheese. That poor first mouse. He had the idea first – to nab that cheese. Where is he now? He's stuck under the wire trap, just in front of the cheese and, sadly, very dead. But the second mouse? Munch, munch! Being first with an idea, product or approach can of course bring benefits. The bigger prize can often await those who bide their time, and then take an idea and make it better.

To win by being second or third, you have to learn to be an outstanding thief. Picasso knew it: '*A good artist copies. A great artist steals!*' Steve Jobs knew it: '*I've been shameless about stealing great ideas*'.

Jogging by the river in Singapore, I stumbled upon the statue of the 'founder' of Singapore, Sir Stamford Raffles. Some dispute whether Sir Stamford actually founded Singapore. It's a moot point. He had a vision for this small fishing port, set the path, and went on to achieve much in his short life. He died aged 46.

Here's the thing: most of Raffles' ideas were not his own. Neither, according to the biography *Raffles and the Golden Opportunity,* were his 'discoveries and his enthusiasms'.

He 'adopted' the ideas of others. *'He picked them up and ran, either carrying them forward himself ... or enabling those with the necessary qualities (to do so.) He had a mind like a magnet, drawing in what caught his imagination and taking it further.'*

That's what I stole from Raffles: a magnet mind.

I have unashamedly 'listened like a thief' all my career, grabbing ideas I have liked and after a tweak or a twist, using them myself. They have stocked my professional and personal tool kit. Sometimes I credit others. Often not. I always encourage anyone to do the same with whatever they can steal from me. Take it. Please. Use it. Make it better. Make it YOURS!

I still do it. Every day. I am constantly alert to what I can take and use. Often I tell people exactly that: *'Hey – that's great. I am going to steal it'*. They laugh. I steal it.

That's life, business and the power of creativity. It's what ideas are all about. Take. Sharpen. Evolve. Use. Attribute. Don't attribute. Over time, I convince myself it was my idea in the first place and it all blurs. My stories are not always 100% true. But stories don't need to be true to be real. Go as hard as you can. And never, ever stop looking for more great stuff you can steal, make better, and make yours.

Postscript

I have done my very best to acknowledge and attribute at the back of this book all the sources of inspiration, ideas, phrases and content that have helped shape my thinking. I know I have missed some. I rip pages out of newspapers and books, or scribble on the back of grocery receipts things I hear or see, and chuck them all into a *Possums* file. Over time, they end up in stories. Often, I just don't recall their sources.

If you spot something you know is not mine and is unattributed, please email me at chris@chrisjohnsavage.com. I will immediately fix it on the master copy so all future online and hard copies of this book have it right. And please – forgive me. It was unintentional. Promise.

1.6
REFRESH YOUR PERSONAL BRAND – FOUR EASY STEPS

If you want to accelerate career growth, then learn these four steps to sharpen your personal brand at work. Do this, and your career will thrive.

Successful consumer brands keep evolving to deliver to current buyers. Think how a BMW has changed in design, mechanics, technology, safety and comfort over the past 10 years. Or how a leading airline keeps evolving its offer to give modern travellers what they need and to keep competitors at bay.

We have to do exactly the same to maintain great 'professional brands' in the minds of our colleagues, and to keep thriving in our careers.

Hugo Boss, Emirates, Audi, Moët et Chandon, Apple. When we hear these brand names, we immediately get a feeling about the product: a perception, made up by many considerations. That's branding.

We're all 'brands', whether we like it or not.

When your name is mentioned in business, those present get an instant feeling about you – their perception of you as a professional brand at that moment in time. Our professional brands are not stagnant: when you start a new role or get promoted, you need to begin again with your brand, and build it afresh.

Here's a powerful, practical four-step model for assessing, nurturing and building professional brands at work, developed by Tom Peters. I loved it when I first read it 10 years ago. I love it even more today. It's practical, and it works.

As you read each of the four pillars, give yourself a score out of 10 with 10/10 being *'I am perceived by my colleagues as BRILLIANT* at this' and 1/10 being *'I am perceived by my colleagues as being absolutely HOPELESS at this'.* Put yourself into the shoes of your colleagues. What do they think of you and this part of your brand? And get input: ask your colleagues and your boss to rate you.

- *Outcomes powerhouse:* I am known as someone who delivers outcomes, who gets things done, who is highly productive on the right things, who delivers on what they say they will do. (How do your colleagues perceive you on this? Give yourself a score out of 10).

- *Expert at something:* I am known for being particularly good at something. While a strong all-rounder, my colleagues perceive me as being an expert in (something) and often seek my counsel in this one area of expertise (score out of 10?).

- *Point of view about the future:* I have a vibrant view on the future (on how to deliver excellently a year away on a client account, on an area of our business that is evolving, on a trend that could impact our business, on a new product offering, and so on). I am thinking ahead and alert to what the future might hold and what we need to do about it (score?).

- *Supportive and trustworthy colleague:* I am known to be trustworthy and supportive. I do not engage in politics, undermine others or gossip. I don't tell lies or claim credit for the work of others. I am transparent and consistent. You know where you stand with me (score?).

Those are the pillars to great personal brands. Score yourself based on how you think OTHERS perceive you. Getting input from colleagues can be helpful, though confronting.

Give it a go. Score yourself. Develop a 100-day 'brand improvement' plan. Get it done. Reassess every three months. Treat yourself as a project! And never stop working on improving and evolving your 'offer'.

1.7
THE BURBERRY COAT, AN ALL BLACK AND FOUR POWERFUL WORDS

I can't get this out of my mind. Could this be the guiding light to living a more fulfilling life, and to catching ourselves before we take the wrong step? Four simple words with a big message.

It was not surprising John was wearing a Burberry trench coat, given he's a senior Burberry leader. We caught up at a local pub. It had been a while. He was overflowing with optimism, enthusiasm and energy.

We talked for three hours. He told me he was reading Richie McCaw's autobiography. Richie is a champion captain of the world's best rugby team, the All Blacks. (If you don't know the sport, think Pelé and Brazil circa 1970, or Michael Jordan and the Chicago Bulls circa early 90s.) McCaw's book held little interest for me.

Then John told me of the advice McCaw's father had given him as an adolescent. It had apparently helped define young Richie's approach to his life. A chill went down my spine. So simple, yet powerful. I can't get it out of my mind. This is what McCaw's father told a young Richie:

Don't let yourself down.

Yip. That's it. So simple and yet so powerful. *Don't let yourself down.* For me, a telling message to keep front of mind, to share with others, to think and act upon. If I ever had a tattoo, this is what it would say: *Don't let yourself down.*

Are you letting yourself down in your career? Could you be pushing harder to learn new skills, challenge yourself, resist complacency, sharpen the value you bring, take on more responsibility, take a risk, ask for a new opportunity, put your hand up, safeguard and nurture relationships? By reading *Savage Oxygen*, you're taking a positive step. Well done!

Are you letting yourself down with your family? Do you give them the time and energy they deserve, are you present, are you a giver rather than a taker, do they get the priority they deserve?

What about your health? Are you listening to your body? Do you give it attention? I read in a gym brochure something like: *'If the car you owned would be your only car for the rest of your life, how would you take care of it?'* Treat your body that way (advice I need to take for myself, that's for sure).

And in your life generally? Remember the words of a business leader who told me: *'The most important things in life can't be measured and can't be bought'.* How are you doing in this regard? Got your act together, or letting yourself down? Are you focused on what is really important to you?

I am thinking hard about what Richie's Dad told him. I'm about to read the book (it was sent to me last week by a senior Nestlé executive who heard me tell this story at a recent speech I did for her team). I want to learn more. I feel it is the best advice a young person could get, and certainly advice that a 54-year-old is not going to ignore. *'Don't let yourself down.'* Think about it.

1.8
THE IRONMAN'S PERFECT SECRET TO SUCCESS

I learnt a tip from an Ironman that has given me hope and confidence. This insight has changed the way I am viewing the challenges facing me in tough times. I have never felt more optimistic. Here's why.

Read the papers. Listen to the news. If you are in business, it's all gloom and doom. Economic woes: businesses under heavy pressure. It's hard not to get pessimistic about the outlook.

Unless, that is, you have heard this advice from former champion Ironman Trevor Hendy. For those not familiar with Ironmen, they are supreme surf lifesavers who also compete in complex surf sport competitions.

I heard the story second hand when presenting some *Possums* highlights to the leadership team of a global consumer products giant. Hendy had spoken to them the week prior. Here's the essence of the message he gave. Hendy says never blame the environment:

Conditions are always perfect.

In Hendy's world, he'd turn up to an Ironman event and see huge waves churning up the surf; or a strong wind coming from the wrong direction; or sweeping rains; or the sea becalmed. It would be easy for an Ironman's shoulders to slump a little when conditions were not in his favour: to feel the chips were against him. *'Don't do it'*, is the thrust of his approach. *'Lift your heads. Conditions are ALWAYS perfect. Get out there and focus on what you can control, and on doing your very best. Back yourselves.'*

'Conditions are always perfect.' It is so easy to use external factors as an excuse; as a reason to talk things down; to give yourself an 'out'; to convince yourself outcomes are beyond your control.

Of course they are a factor and that is reality. But, change your mindset.

Take the approach that whatever the conditions and circumstance, they are perfect for you to do your best, outsmart your competition, thrill a prospect and achieve your goals. Follow these four guidelines:

- *Keep your mind positive* by accepting complete responsibility for yourself and everything that happens to you.
- *Refuse to criticise* or blame others.
- *Resolve to make progress* rather than excuses.
- *Keep your energy focused forward* on the things you CAN improve in your business and your life.

Conditions are ALWAYS perfect. And conditions are perfect right now to gain ideas and insights from this book to help evolve, grow and be the very best you can be – at work and in your life. You've made a start: now – keep going!

Postscript

Olympic gold medal-winning British rowers apparently use the expression: *'That's outside my boat'*. This is how they describe everything that happens outside of their control (e.g. the weather). They are only interested in what they can control – what is 'inside the boat'. Always focus on improving the things you can control. Conditions are always perfect!

LEADERSHIP LESSONS FROM THE FRONT LINE

Whether you are leading a company, account service team, client relationship, or even if you are leading a team of one – yourself – then these 12 leadership lessons and the stories that expand on each will be of real value. Read them chronologically, or just dip in and out – up to you! Each tells a story about how to lead yourself, your teams and your business to greater success in a fast changing world.

2.1
TAKE ACTION

2.1 A
THE MOST CRITICAL CHARACTERISTIC OF LEADERSHIP

It's said cream rises to the top. Must also be true of sour cream, because inevitably I have ended up a key leader in whatever I have done, throughout my life. Bizarre. How could that be? Why me? I now have the answer.

I'll never forget being appointed leader of the Life of an Ant project team, aged eight, at Camps Bay Primary School in 1967. I can still hear the sound of my feet hitting the floorboards as I swaggered, 10 feet tall, across the room to the corner where my team was to group. I liked the feeling of being in charge.

It's been that way ever since. Whether at school, sports teams, and for the past 30 years in business, I have been asked to be – or just ended up as – either the leader, or a key leader.

Why do leaders end up leading? I don't believe people are 'born leaders'. So what is it they do that sees them placed in positions of authority? Well, I found out the other day when I read this quote on a bus ticket:

A leader is one who knows what needs to be done, and then has the courage to get on and do it.

Put another way: *a leader is someone who knows where he or she wants to go, and gets up and goes.* Knowing is not enough. You must take action. Hope is not a plan.

Former Australian prime minister Paul Keating defines leadership as: *'The combination of imagination and courage'.* I like that. Former Telstra senior executive Phil Burgess told me: *'Character is action'.*

Point is, the first characteristic of leadership is to take action. I believe action brings clarity. Get started and the clarity will come. Tom Peters describes it something like: *'Ready ... FIRE! FIRE! FIRE! Aim'.*

Former colleague, Mike Howorth, debates this. He believes clarity brings action. Be clear on what you are trying to achieve and that will spur you into action.

This Japanese proverb suggests they both have a point: *'Vision without action is a dream. Action without vision is a nightmare'.*

Either way, whatever works for you: Take Action.

It is the first and most important characteristic of leadership. And a critical pillar of success.

2.1 B
ONE GIFT FACEBOOK GAVE ME THAT MADE A REAL DIFFERENCE

I am not really a Facebook user. I have a *Possums* Facebook page, and appreciate its role, but have yet to be convinced I need it more pervasively in my life. That was until I learnt this one tip from Facebook. It's brilliant! I use it every day. Bet you will too.

I am a private person (*Possums* is the exception, and is about sharing, learning and keeping 'current'). I don't want other people knowing what I or my family are doing. I love my friends and extended family, but don't feel the need to know too much about their daily lives either. If they need help, I am there. If we're together, I am present and enthused. Apart from that, I don't need regular communication (apart from with my mum of course).

So I have never really 'got' Facebook. I understand why others embrace it, and respect that (apart from those addicted to 'bragging' on Facebook about how awesome they and their lives are – you know who you are) but it leaves me cold. That was until I learnt that on the reception wall at Facebook's head office is a quote, which I now use every day. Here it is:

Done is better than perfect.

Get stuff 'done' and move on.

Now, many colleagues whom I respect have vigorously disagreed with me about this concept. They take the view: *'Don't let good be the enemy of great'*. In other words, go the extra yard and make sure anything you do is as good as you can do it. I get that.

In the incredibly busy and pressured lives we lead, adopting this next mantra has helped keep me highly productive, making progress and moving forward: *'Don't let the search for perfection be the enemy of the good'*.

Sometimes you have to say: *'Enough already – wrap it up, move on'*. Whether it's an email you're writing, an article you're editing, a change you're trying to drive through: whatever. It is easy to get stuck on something, fine-tuning and striving for perfection.

As General George S. Patton said: *'A good plan, violently executed now, is better than a perfect plan next week'*. After all, as Mike Tyson said: *'Everyone has a plan until they are punched in the face'*. Love that! Take action before the punch comes!

The fact is, to make a real difference in most of what we need to do, *'done is better than perfect'*.

Have the courage to take action, make progress and then move on. It makes a huge difference to your output and effectiveness. (Okay, enough editing already. Move on, Chris.)

2.1 C
THE 'DYNAMIC DUO' TO DRIVE YOUR SUCCESS

There are two forces at play that must be working in partnership if you are to achieve big goals. I've only just discovered this. It is already making a huge difference in my life.

Look in the mirror and you will see your best friend and your greatest enemy. When I see me in that mirror, I shake my head in dismay, wonderment and bemusement at what an oddity I am. Strong, decisive, able in many ways, yet weak, flawed, broken in so many others.

What baffles me most is how I am often able to take action and achieve some goals, and yet fail so miserably on others, even though I try multiple ways of tackling them. I now have the answer:

Goals are achieved when we have two forces at play: desire and willpower.

When properly combined, they make an irresistible pair. (This is a little dry but magical. Stick with it.)

Desire: You have to really, really want something. You have to have the *hunger*.

Willpower: You have to have *self-discipline,* which comes through self-control. You must first control yourself. And self-mastery is the hardest job you will ever tackle. You have to have *resolve*.

Here's a superb definition of self-discipline. *'Doing what you need to do, when you need to do it, even when you don't want to.'* Pause. Reflect. Read that again.

Self-discipline leads to habits. Habits lead to persistence. Persistence leads to results. (Lack of persistence is one of the major causes of failure – usually the habit of quitting when overtaken by temporary setbacks.)

Here's the learning. I have always put my focus on the willpower bit. The self-discipline and resolve, built on self-control, that leads to habits, then to persistence, and then results. The 'how'.

I fail to achieve goals not because of the willpower. Sure, the willpower fails. That's a symptom. The cause of failure in willpower is due to a lack of a powerful 'why'. It's all about weak **desire**. I simply have not 'wanted it enough'.

The starting point of all achievement is DESIRE. We have to focus our energies up front, on the intensity of the desire. Weak desires bring weak results.

If you want to achieve goals, your first action is to spend time on the WHY. Make sure you have a clear vision of what success looks and feels like. As you push hard along the path of willpower towards delivering on that goal, check in regularly on the DESIRE. Savour victory. Imagine it. Feel it. Taste it. Bathe in it. Breathe it in.

Then get back on the willpower path: self-discipline delivering habits, then persistence, and then results.

Print out this story. Laminate it. Stick it in your shower. Read it every day. DESIRE. It's the starting point of all achievement.

Postscript

I bought a book by Napoleon Hill at the airport in Ho Chi Minh City. I'd often seen quotes attributed to him, but had not read any of his works. Two hours later on the plane to Singapore, the guy next to me asked how I was finding the book. *'Hard going,'* I replied. *'It's a dull read.'* He laughed. *'Persistence, my friend. There will be magic in there for you.'* I read on. He was right. In the final pages I stumbled upon the desire and willpower insight. I got the 'magic' because I 'turned up' for myself. I read on, pushing through the dullness to the gem. Just 'turning up'. It's 85% of the secret to success.

2.1 D
A PRICE OF LEADERSHIP –
NOW IS THE TIME FOR YOU TO PAY IT

It's Anzac Day, the annual remembrance of those fallen in Australia's conflicts. In watching the documentaries of war stories and legends, I revisit my dark secret. You see, I am a coward at heart. Big time.

I look at what those men and women did, risked, attempted and then think about how I would act in similar circumstances. In truth, I can't imagine anything except terror, self-preservation and ducking for cover.

In the face of great threat and unimaginable horror, ordinary people do find the courage to step up: to perform amazing acts of bravery, to risk all to help and protect others, to show leadership under fire. Many paid the ultimate price for that. Lest we forget.

Not wanting to trivialise war and sacrifice, I do take a powerful leadership lesson from this reality. Respectfully, here it is:

The cost of leadership is self-interest.

Author and motivational speaker Simon Sinek puts it something like this: *'We are happy for our leaders to get perks. But when danger comes, we expect them to take action and to run towards the danger: to put themselves at risk to protect us'.*

You have heard this before: every business is under unprecedented attack as technology changes everything. This fundamental 'game change' is happening everywhere. The barbarians ARE at the gate.

So, if you lead a team, an account, a P&L, an office, a division – if you are a leader – are you taking action and running towards the danger?

Are you putting yourself in the shoes of those out there who are thinking today about how to steal your client, your account, your team, your business? Are you thinking about solutions, no matter what personal risk might be involved?

To 'step up' you must have the courage to tell hard truths to powerful others who often don't want to hear it. Just because they don't like the message does not mean it is not true.

Be prepared for the possibility that your ideas might not be right. At least have them – air them – see if your clients, partners and colleagues are prepared to consider and debate them. Speak up. Speak with candour – truth without malice. Agitate for debate. Drive restless and relentless thinking and questioning about what's coming, and how we must adapt and adopt to thrive tomorrow. Remember:

- The cost of leadership is self-interest.

- Run towards the danger facing your area of responsibility.

- Have the courage to tell those who need to know the hard truths.

- Be prepared that your ideas might not be right – but at least have them.

Most of the stories of the greatest bravery and self-sacrifice from conflicts are not about generals and field marshals. They are about rank and file, who had the courage to see the threat, or the opportunity, and to take action. Sometimes they provided the spear for advance: other times, the shield to protect. They stood up. And often paid the price. Lest we forget.

We don't have to face the mortal dangers the Anzacs did. We do have the opportunity to protect others in our little worlds at a time of threat. Have you got the courage to run towards the danger? Do you? Do I? Let's see …

2.1 E
NIKE AND THE F WORD:
HOW TO MOTIVATE YOURSELF INTO ACTION

Warning! This story contains a naughty word. It starts with F and ends with K. But it's a relevant aspect to a story that has had an immediate, dramatic and positive impact on my effectiveness, productivity and ability to take action.

Productive, successful executives are those able to consistently tackle and complete difficult and big challenges. It's a constant struggle for me. How do they do it?

I've now learnt a great tip from a book by fitness guru Michelle Bridges, who made her name as the fitness coach on the TV show, *The Biggest Loser.* Michelle's advice is this:

JFDI – Just Fucking Do It! (But there's a twist. Read on!)

In motivating her clients to exercise, her approach was this: when you wake up at 6am for your run, and it's dark and cold and you're convincing yourself to get back into bed, don't. Instead, JFDI, and make this deal with yourself: just commit to exercising for 10 minutes. If after that time you still don't feel like doing it, then return home and put the kettle on. That's the deal. JFDI … for 10 minutes.

Michelle reports she has had some of her best ever workouts when she's adopted JFDI, making a deal with herself that if after 10 minutes she still wants to go back to bed, she can. Once you start, and get 10 minutes under the belt, you're on a roll, and you'll keep going. Guaranteed!

Here's the lesson for each of us.

Do you have a big new business proposal to write? Client meeting your team wants you to go to but you really, really don't feel like it? A stack of staff appraisal forms to complete? Often it seems like the more important the task, the harder is it to get started. So, to get more of the difficult and big challenges done, faster:

- *Identify your Big Rock:* Identify your most critical, 'must do' task every day. I call this my Big Rock.

- *Start the day with it:* Plan so you are able to make a start on your Big Rock first thing, or as soon as possible, the next day.

- *Prepare the night before:* If possible, assemble whatever you will need to make a start on your Big Rock – documents, research reports, phone numbers. Clear your desk except for these items.

- *JFDI:* Make a start as soon as you get to work, and if you're really not in the mood, just commit to doing it for 10 minutes.

SURPRISE! You got it done – again! I am using JFDI several times a day now. Every time that voice says *'Nah, do it later'*, another voice says *'Nah, I'll JFDI instead'*. Give it a go. It works!

2.2

SET ACHIEVABLE, SHORT-TERM GOALS

2.2 A
EIGHT STEPS TO DELIVER A WORLD-CLASS RESULT – EVERY TIME

When we staged our annual kick-off conference for 400 leaders, the feedback was outstanding. *'The most inspiring, impressive conference day of my career.' 'Better than TED, better than the Cannes Creativity Festival.'* How had we pulled off such a triumph?

What the project team did in that first hour of the planning ensured the success of this event. It's a tip proven to deliver outstanding results when there's a major goal to achieve.

Begin with the end in mind.

It's one of Steven Covey's 7 Habits of Highly Effective People from his book of the same name, and it works. Dammit – IT WORKS!

We started the first planning session, three months earlier, by working through, minute-by-minute, how the day would unfold. We started with the look and feel of the stage. Then what would happen when leaders arrived at the venue. How we'd get them into the theatre. What would be on screen as they walked in. The lighting. The music. We called it our 'screenplay'.

We started the project with absolute clarity about what success looked like. We began with the end very much in our sights. A goal without a plan is just a wish. We had both a goal and a plan.

Bill Marsteller defined excellence this way: *'Clarity of purpose, attention to detail'*. Remember, excellence is a habit. We had clarity from the start as to what we wanted to achieve. To deliver, we turned to the proven 8 Step Delivering Excellence formula:

- Determine what you are striving to achieve – have a vivid image of it

- Write down that outcome, in the past tense, as if you've achieved it: *'Today we held a leadership meeting hailed by our leaders as outstanding'*

- Write down the date you want to be able to say this.

- Brainstorm a long list of everything you need to do to achieve that result .

- Develop a plan – phase the work based on priorities.

- Allocate responsibilities.

- Set short-term goals and milestones, with clear deadlines.

- Get started immediately.

We also paid big attention to rehearsing. In fact, we rehearsed the rehearsals to ensure content and linkages were perfect before the final run through. Then we did a dress rehearsal. Every step of the way. Frame by frame.

And what a day it was. At 8pm that day, after an avalanche of glowing feedback, we were able to say: *'Today we held a leadership meeting hailed by our leaders as outstanding'*.

It all started by beginning with the end in mind. It works – every time!

2.2 B
THE POWER OF SMALL STEPS

'Success is steady progress towards one's personal goals.' That's what my fortune cookie from the Peacock Gardens restaurant in Sydney told me.

Achieving goals can be a daunting journey, littered with setbacks. Here's a tip that has helped me dust myself off when I've failed. It works, whatever your age.

My eight-year-old mate was learning to play rugby. This season the boys had to tackle each other. In the first game, he did all he could to avoid tackling. *'You have to tackle,'* I yelled at him during the game, and continued to hound him with the same mantra during the following week. Saturday came around and despite all the counselling, cajoling, encouragement and good intentions, not one tackle! If I had hair, I would have pulled it out.

A local fitness trainer gave me this advice: *'Ask him to do just two really good tackles in the next game. He needs to know he does not need to do any more once he's done two'.* I explained this to my mate. He was perplexed. But agreed. Next game, he made two great tackles, and avoided any more. Progress! The following week, we asked for four tackles. He delivered four, and no more. The next week, six tackles were duly made. At time of writing, we're a day away from an eight-tackle game. That takes him to half time! And the rest, as they say, is history.

Here is the learning. The habit I have learnt to help achieve goals is this:

Set manageable, short-term targets along the way.

Always begin with the end in mind. Have clarity around the big picture goal. Then set a time frame. *'I want to be a great tackler by game five.'* *'I want my firm to win the XYZ account by Christmas.'* *'I want to be promoted to account director by September 30.'* Then set manageable targets: step-by-step goals within our reach.

Achieve big goals *'two tackles at a time'*. When you accomplish goals, you gain confidence and momentum. In this way, you give yourself regular 'wins' along the way, and inspire yourself to keep going.

Progress, no matter how small, is to be applauded. Success is, after all, just the sum of small efforts, repeated day in and day out.

Postscript

Brian Tracy tells this story in *Eat That Frog*. A North African country had two towns separated by 500 miles of featureless desert. Sand would blow over tyre tracks between the towns every night. This was pre-GPS days! As more trucks tried to travel between the two towns, they'd often get lost. People were dying.

Local officials painted 100 oil barrels black, drove between the towns, and every five miles they'd position one barrel and fill it with sand. When done, 100 black oil drums lined the path from town A to town B, five miles apart.

To get from town A to town B, you did not have to focus on the entire, daunting journey (even though you knew exactly where you wanted to get to). You just had to focus on the next oil barrel. Then the next. And so on. Before you knew it, you were 50 oil barrels in and halfway there.

Begin with the end in mind: be clear about what you want to achieve. Then achieve big goals 'one oil barrel' or 'two tackles' at a time by setting manageable, short-term targets.

2.2 C
HOW TO ACHIEVE GOALS –
BUT DON'T TELL ANYONE THIS SECRET

I have let myself down badly – again. I look in the mirror and shake my head in dismay. How could you do this, Chris? Then I read the answer, in the autobiography of a British Hollywood actor of old. It's a wake-up call for me, and for you.

David Niven's *The Moon's a Balloon* was a gem to read en route to Los Angeles and with Hollywood to be explored. He recounts his time spent with Winston Churchill during the gloomy early days of the Second World War. Churchill kept reassuring Niven about '*... when the Americans join us ...*' Suddenly, Pearl Harbour happened, and the Americans joined the war. '*How did you know this would happen?*' an incredulous Niven asked the great man. '*Because, my boy, I am a great student of history.*' Point is, Churchill knew reluctant bystanders usually get drawn into conflict. History predicted it.

In that statement I realised why I keep failing, time and again, on simple personal goals. Here's why.

I am insane. I believe by doing the same thing over and over again, I'll get a different outcome.

I need to be a student of history. If my way failed in the past, why should it succeed now? History suggests the way I go about achieving certain personal goals is deeply flawed. In this instance, it's about weight loss and fitness. Here's the sad story. I had a health scare and committed to getting fit and dropping weight.

Mistake number one: I did what I always do

Off I went on a massive diet and exercise 'campaign' brutalising myself to achieve weekly goals; writing down every session; consulting graphs, heart monitors, things that go 'beep' – the works.

The weight dropped off. It usually does. 12 kilos in two months. 10 more to go. I was feeling great, looking good and loving the feedback! *'Wow, Chris, you're well on your way to achieving your goals. WELL DONE!!'* Then I was in Asia, exercising daily. The last day was at a conference in rural Thailand. It does not get hotter or more humid. During the lunch break, I ran for an hour. Madness. Flew home. Fell sick. Off-colour and no exercise for three weeks. Got out of the habit and became despondent. Ate and drank. 10 kilos back on. In just eight weeks!

Mistake number two: I shared my goal far and wide

This is the mistake (and insight) I just learnt via a TED video, of a guy who said this: *'To achieve your goals, don't tell anyone about them'.* I have always believed the opposite. If I tell those around me, then they hold me accountable to deliver. Not true, says the research. Those who share goals feel an almost instant sense of having achieved part of the journey. As people start giving them encouragement and feedback, they feel they are well on their way. It is then easier to convince yourself to ease up as you think *'I am basically there'.*

Rather, keep goals totally private. Then quietly work away until you have achieved them.

So, two lessons from a once-again failed, or should I say 'stalled', fitness and weight loss campaign:

- *Learn from history:* If the way you go about it has not worked in the past, why the hell will it work now?

- *Keep your goals to yourself:* Write down the goal, with a deadline, make a long list of everything you need to do to achieve it, develop a prioritised plan, and get on with it. But only tell yourself.

2.2 D
YOU WON'T EXPECT THIS PROVEN WAY TO ACHIEVE GOALS

Feeding (pun intended) off the previous story, I have tried every diet under the sun. Sadly, my self-discipline has never been strong enough to achieve long-term results. One time though I did really well. The reason is a great lesson for achieving goals.

Okay. I know it simply comes down to eating less and moving more. Easier said than done. For me, anyway. I comfort eat. Balloon out. Then I do a weight loss 'blitz', lose 10 kilos, feel great, get busy, get stressed, and kapow! Those jeans I put in the 'throw out' pile as they were hanging off the 'new' me ... well, they are back on, top button undone as it can't be done up.

One system did have a longer-term effect. Weight Watchers. It really did work, until I stopped going to the weekly meetings. In that statement is the magic to achieving goals.

People do what is inspected, not what is expected.

Weight Watchers works (for me anyway) because you turn up every week to be weighed, by a stranger, with your result up there for all to see. I made damned sure I'd get a great weekly result. There was nowhere to hide. I had to face the numbers every week. And I made sure they went down, every week.

It's a phenomenon called the Hawthorne effect. Subjects improve or modify an aspect of their behaviour, which is being experimentally measured or monitored, in response to the fact they know they are being studied.

It's the same as when I use a personal trainer. My effort and results go through the roof. I am being monitored. Measured. I want to get positive feedback, to do well. I put it in, much harder than I ever would if I was doing it alone, with no-one watching, no-one monitoring.

I read on a fitness blog that the highest ranked tip given by a large cohort of fitness trainers on how to achieve goals was simply this: get a buddy. In other words, get someone to share the journey with you.

So, here's the message: get a 'conscience'.

Set yourself achievable, short-term goals that are regularly measured and reviewed by someone whose views you care about.

The weird thing is, it works! The longer you have the self-discipline to keep the system going – reviewing, fine-tuning, acknowledging, rewarding, recalibrating – the better the results. Give it a go. It might just give you that extra nudge you need.

2.3
FACE REALITY

2.3 A
HAVE COURAGE – ONE MAGICAL HABIT FOR YOUR BUSINESS (AND LIFE)

One of our leaders took what many would feel was a big risk last week. He asked for an 'urgent' meeting, where he then outlined why his business was in 'deep trouble'. We left the meeting delighted. Huh?

You see, we concluded this business was NOT in deep trouble. It had strength and vitality, with great people and deep specialisation. It had simply drifted away from its 'heartland', from what it did best. By playing again to its strengths, it would thrive.

What excited us most was the pace of progress made in the discussion. This was made possible by all in the room doing one thing. It's hard to do, but if you form the habit, incredibly refreshing and invigorating.

Face reality – always!

Former General Electric CEO Jack Welch was passionate about 'facing reality'. He drove this habit through the way he ran his businesses, and the culture he built. Face reality. Look hard at a situation and see what is really there. And then tell the truth.

It is human nature to gloss over bad news. We all do it. Steve Jobs was a master at it: if he did not like a reality he *'just put it out of his mind and ignored it'*. The reality does not go away. Business writer Margaret Heffernan calls it *'wilful blindness'* – why we ignore the obvious at our peril. Here are three ways to make 'facing reality' a habit:

- *Celebrate and share your stuff-ups*

'Executives must be able to advocate for the truth,' says Paul Gibson from Royal Melbourne Institute of Technology. Create a culture where sharing failure – being open and frank – is real. I have always shared my stuff-ups, taking valuable lessons from them. I've also encouraged teams to share theirs, far and wide. We learn more from these stories than from hearing of triumphs.

- *Reward outstanding management of failure*

Reward staff on their ability to identify and manage issues or failure. Setbacks are inevitable. Things will go wrong. Reward the ability to see that, and the courage to face it, address it, make further change. You have to be prepared to make a mistake if you are to build success.

- *'Retreat slowly'*

The biggest mistake I made with bosses of old was to 'face reality' and then present a new financial forecast that showed a big decline. That's not helpful. And usually not necessary. Instead, 'retreat slowly'. Face reality, see the problems, and then work hard at addressing them while protecting financial performance and minimising decline. This might mean slowing down another initiative, delaying hires, postponing discretionary spend, or driving hard for extra revenues elsewhere. (While 'retreat slowly' is an excellent compass point, it's also wise, on occasion, to heed the advice of Sun Tzu: *'Sometimes the best strategy is just to run away'*).

Face reality. Look hard at a situation. Tell the truth. Then take action fast and decisively.

Postscript

Here's a story, stolen from several advertising industry leaders: from Tom Moult, who stole it from Jon Steel, who stole it from Jeremy Bullmore. Jeremy was apparently travelling on a Canadian Airlines flight. On landing, the aircraft slammed on to the runway with a terrible bang. Passengers screamed. Some cried. The plane screeched to a halt. Quite reasonably, the panicked, anxious passengers awaited the explanation from the captain. What had happened? Had a tyre burst? Had they hit an animal on landing? What could explain that terrible bang, and heavy braking? The public address system crackled into life: *'This is Captain Johnson speaking. I've been flying with Canadian for more than thirty years, and that was the worst fucking landing I've ever made!'*

Here's the surprise: the captain was suddenly a hero. As the passengers left the plane, they all wanted to shake his hand; they probably wanted to fly with him again. Why? Because in a world of squirrelly explanations, he'd been disarmingly honest. He'd faced reality, and told the truth.

2.3 B
ARE YOU BRAVE ENOUGH TO TRY THIS? NOT SURE I AM

Here's something I am terrible at, and often petrified by. It's uncomfortable. Yet this one simple habit makes for better leadership and relationships. It can also be disastrous, if mismanaged. I am determined to improve. It won't be easy. Are you brave enough to join me? Truthfully?

All my life I have struggled with this one trait. Maybe it was the fear of hurting other people's feelings? Or that somehow I'd look bad or inadequate if I did it. I've dodged it whenever I can, or approached it in an obtuse, circular fashion.

A good mentor does it well. I have role models. Still I struggle to do this one thing consistently. I bet you struggle to do this too.

Speak with candour.

Candour is, after all, telling the truth without malice. Not that I tell the truth with malice. I just don't always tell the truth. It's not that I tell lies. I just don't always speak out, to state my beliefs, objections, true thoughts – bravely and firmly.

I got thinking about this when I read Richard Sauerman's (@the_brand_guy on Twitter) post about 'speak up': *'Speaking up is simply an honest expression of our thoughts and feelings,'* he writes. I read that with a sinking heart. I realised I often don't speak up: to express my views genuinely and fully.

Some who know me will dispute this: *'Come on Chris, that's rubbish. You're provocative and blunt'.* That's true, some of the time. Often though I am simply afraid to say what I feel. I don't know why. I just am.

I am going to make a big effort to speak with candour this year: to tell the truth without malice, with clients, colleagues, friends and relatives. This will also include not misrepresenting things about myself to put myself in a better light, or to cover my butt. I have tentatively begun the journey. So far so good. It is actually invigorating.

Do you speak with candour? Be candid now. If not, will you join me in trying to improve this year?

Postscript

Am I being hypocritical in saying that, sometimes, it's okay to tell a fib? For example, to manage your communication when you know that candour – truth without malice – is going to be counter-productive and will unnecessarily hurt feelings? I reckon it's okay to tell a fib in those circumstances. We all know those occasions – *'does my bum look big in these jeans?'* moments. So while I will be trying hard to 'speak up', I'll also do it sensibly and sensitively.

2.3 C
THE FIRST RULE OF CRISIS MANAGEMENT –
USE IT EVERY DAY!

A tumour was found on my vocal chords. I walked from the specialist's surgery to my office and for the next four hours devoted myself to the first rule of crisis management. It helped me then, and helps me every day – in business and in life. Do you do it?

Imagine you were advising the mayor of Toronto (at the time of writing, this guy was in a real crisis due to his bad behaviour). An allegation of substance abuse is made. All hell breaks loose. What do you do next?

Remember what actually happened? First, the video of him taking crack cocaine appeared, with an online auction grabbing headlines as to who would buy the tape. Evidence of public drunkenness emerged. Then prostitutes. Drink driving. More illegal drugs. I mean: oi fricking vey!

If you'd been advising this guy, the first rule of crisis management was an absolute MUST!

Always plan for the worst case – for more bad news.

In crisis management, experience suggests the crisis WILL get worse. A great crisis team immediately splits. While some address the crisis, others immediately scenario-plan what could go wrong next and how to respond should that occur. By anticipating escalation of the problem, you are ready to tackle it, quickly, efficiently, calmly – thereby minimising damage. Having 'worst case' plans gives you confidence to get on with immediate priorities.

Whenever you are about to do something where you fear a significant repercussion, plan for the bad news. Here's what to do:

- *Think about the potential worst-case scenarios:* The client fired us; I got fired; that leader has quit and left the building immediately; three on a team resigned in protest to a decision; my boyfriend dumped me; I have cancer and have a fight ahead. Whatever it is, think clearly about the worst that could happen.

- *Plan what you would do if that happened:* Write down all the options.

- *Develop an action plan:* Be specific about what you would do, step by step, to handle that worst case should it actually happen.

- *Put the plan in a drawer:* Lift your shoulders. Go forth and tackle the situation head on. Remain absolutely positive – but face reality of the worst case first, and have your plans ready.

I am not promoting 'catastrophising'. As Michel de Montaigne said: *'There were many terrible things in my life, but most of them never happened'.* This is about managing the anxiety of the unknown. Once you have a worst-case plan, you can relax. It's like insurance.

What's the worst that can happen? As I did when that specialist rang after the tumour biopsy to say: *'All clear – benign',* you open the drawer, and tear up the plan. (In this case the plan I had made was the steps to take if I had cancer, and on securing my family's financial security should I die).

Confidence is preparation. Plan for the worst case.

2.3 D
THE MOST IMPORTANT HUMAN NEED –
JUST ASK THOSE ON DEATH ROW

I learnt a big lesson through adversity these past weeks. It reminded me of something we need if we are to be at our best – at work, with relationships, in life. It's simple. It's something so devastating when it's not there.

In Japan, there was a time when those on death row were burdened with what survivors reported was a fate worse than death. In that system, you were told you were to die, but not when. In some cases, death row inmates sat out 20 years awaiting their fate. Whenever they heard footsteps approaching their cell, that could be the moment they would die. The footsteps passed the door – they lived another hour, another day. Imagine living that way, for 20 years!

I was reminded this week of the devastating power one simple state of being, and word, can have on our lives and ability to perform at our best.

Uncertainty – it destroys our confidence. Certainty – it underpins and accelerates confidence.

Have you ever been 'paralysed with doubt'? That's uncertainty screwing you up.

What we want most is certainty. We can deal with certainty. But constantly wondering *'Will it, or won't it?'* is genuinely debilitating.

I got the reminder as medical test after test could not pinpoint the cause of pain in my gut. I trawled the internet to self-diagnose (a disastrous thing to do!). I speculated and fretted, always concluding a worst case. I became 'paralysed with doubt'. The doctors then speculated gall bladder. Out it came. The pathology report: *'Rotten gall bladder. Worst we have seen!'*

Certainty. Done and dusted. Get on with it.

Will you be picked for the team? No. Okay – certainty. I can deal with that. Will I get that new job? Yes! Onwards! Start planning. Is my boss happy with my work? Or not? ASK HER! Get clarity. Certainty. Are we delivering to the client's expectations or are they considering re-pitching? Do a feedback session. Get a reality check done. Get certainty. Am I sick and will I die? Want to stay in that state of uncertainty, or get an answer? I vote for certainty. Every time.

Sometimes uncertainty is created by the pace we work at, and the amount we try to do. We get overwhelmed. Simplify. Simplicity gives us certainty, and certainty we can deal with.

I can deal with setbacks and disappointment. But there is nothing to be gained from uncertainty. It eats away at you, puts you on edge, erodes confidence, and is an insidious enemy.

Push for certainty. Then move forward with confidence, no matter what path you must take.

2.4
SHARPEN YOUR JUDGMENT

2.4 A
THE RABBI, JESUS AND LE RAT: SOLVING A LEADERSHIP DILEMMA

I was at the bat mitzvah of the daughter of Jewish friends. The rabbi told a story about Jesus. *'Eureka!'* I yelled in my head on hearing it. *'That's the answer to the hardest skill emerging leaders have to master.'* Here it is.

It's all about judgment. We are given leadership positions because our bosses trust our judgment – that at key moments, when nobody's watching, we will make the right call. It's impossible to teach 'judgment'. It comes naturally to some, and usually evolves with experience.

The biggest barrier to would-be leaders getting promoted is perceived lack of sound judgment. I have never known how to coach individuals to develop their judgment. Until I heard this story, as told by the rabbi. It is exactly what young leaders need to know if they want to be entrusted with more senior roles.

'A Christian minister was guiding a young man on how to lead a Christian life. "Here," he said. "I have made you a wristband with 'WWJD?' written on it. It stands for What Would Jesus Do? Every time you have to make a decision on how to behave or what to do, ask yourself: What Would Jesus Do? And use that as your guide." 'So,' said the rabbi, 'I want to talk today about WWAJD? What Would A Jew Do?' And he went on to discuss Jewish values. It's the concept I love.

Who is your most powerful role model?

Whose judgment do you most admire and place real stock in? A parent, an early boss, or a great leader like Nelson Mandela? In your mind, create that wristband: WWDD? What Would Dad Do? WWPD? What Would Paula Do? WWND? What Would Nelson Do?

As you work in the daily trenches and tricky issues emerge needing your judgment call, check in with your figurative role model. *'Hang on – what would Dad (Paula, Nelson and so on) do?'* Use that imaginary sounding board as a reality check on the decision you are about to make.

I was telling Russ about this. He runs Junior, a communications business in Brisbane. *'Nothing new there, Chris,'* Russ replied. *'At Junior we have had 'WWLRD?' for years. It guides everything we do.'* 'What the heck is WWLRD?' I asked.

'What Would Le Rat Do?' he replied. *'In solving a client issue, we challenge thinking by bringing rat cunning to it. Le Rat is the most cunning thinker around. We problem-solve from the perspective of Le Rat. It helps us develop sharper, more powerful ideas.'*

Adopt a figurative role model, someone who can be by your side as an invisible sounding board at all times. Create that imaginary wristband. It will help your judgment. Wish I had thought of that 30 years ago.

Postscript

Picasso was an old man. Sitting in a restaurant, a woman rushed up to him: *'My God, you're Picasso! Please – scribble me a drawing on this serviette'*. This he did in a quick 20-second flourish. As he handed it to her, he said: *'Madame, here it is. That will be $100,000 please'*. *'Oh, but you must be joking, Mr Picasso. That's ridiculous! That drawing only took you but a few seconds.'* *'No Madame,'* he replied. *'It took me 84 years to do that.'* Nothing builds insight, ability and judgment more than hard-fought experience and battle scars.

2.4 B
WHY WE ALL NEED A JUSTUS IN OUR LIVES

Justus died the day before I was to have lunch with him. His death struck me hard. Not only because I'd miss him. But because I realised how lucky I had been to have him in my life, for one year, 15 years earlier.

When Justus came into my life, I did not want him in it. He was appointed my chairman, with a brief to keep me under control. I saw him as a spy. He was a tough, opinionated, seasoned former big-time CEO. A Dutchman. Dogmatic. I deeply resented his forced intrusion into my world.

Then I began to look forward to being with him. Justus listened to me. He made suggestions – not directly, but by sharing his experiences in similar circumstances. I began to look up to him; to want to impress him. I became hungry for his approval.

When I decided to resign from that phase of my career, it was Justus I told first. He understood. He embraced me. We kept in touch ever since. Justus had been for me, for that one tough year, the most valuable asset we can have. He was my:

Mentor – a wise and trusted counsellor and teacher.

Mentors are different to coaches. A mentor is an influential senior sponsor and supporter. A coach gives instruction and advice, and is usually well experienced in your industry. A mentor can come from any walk of life. Both have a role.

Houston's Stuart O'Brien: *'A mentor recognises something in you that reminds them of themselves at your age. They keep good people on the right track. They shape you without your knowing it'.*

Former Canning's CEO John Hurst: *'The magic comes in their ability for 30 minutes to focus entirely on you. They help you face reality. They help shape your judgment, but do it in a careful way'.*

STW's Mike Connaghan: *'My key mentor always seemed to know when to pat me on the back when I needed positive feedback. It lifted me when I needed it.'*

Australian Rugby Union's John Nicholl: *'I am reminded by my friend Chris White, a manager of elite athletes, who says: "I am the only one telling them what they need to hear, not what they want to hear." A good mentor tells you what you need to hear'*.

Former TMS CEO Chris Mort: *'A mentor is a great teacher. Mine taught me many things: how and when to take shortcuts, how to make tough decisions, how timing was everything. He never did it for you, but showed you the path'*.

I went on a corporate event where we were paired with sports stars from a national sporting team. We were to become their 'mentors' (for those who know this sport, I got Wendell Sailor and Lote Tuqiri!). That does not work. You can't 'select' a mentor. I get requests *'to be my mentor'* and I always say no.

Mentoring relationships evolve. You often don't even realise someone is or has been a mentor to you until the time has passed. Looking back you can see the influence and role they had.

If you have a mentor, celebrate. Nurture them. Relish in it. I have found mentoring relationships have an end date: you evolve, or the mentor moves on. New mentors materialise. And that's okay.

Mentors help you develop your self-awareness and your judgment, and that gift stays with you always.

Postscript

When I resigned from my Burson-Marsteller career in 1999, Justus gave me a gift: a bottle of Grange Hermitage with, handwritten on the label, *'In friendship ... Justus'*. He fell ill soon afterwards, and battled cheerfully for 14 years with a debilitating health regimen. I will never open that bottle, but will keep it in view always. In friendship. Justus thank you.

2.4 C
MY WEEKEND FROM HELL – A LESSON FOR ALL

I have spent an awful weekend – in total dismay at how I could have let myself and others down so badly. I can't believe I made the same mistake again. It is unforgivable. Really. I have failed. It's a sad story.

I am always ready to tell all how brilliant and wise I am, and how I have learnt so many great lessons in my 30 years in business.

So I need to fess up when I screw up. Today I have my head bowed and tail firmly between my legs. I failed to learn from the past. I forgot the lessons of previous stuff-ups. We have to learn from our mistakes, and not make them again. Yet I did exactly that – and I am ashamed by it. Here's the massive mistake I made. In fact, there are two of them.

I failed to trust my instincts – and I failed to face reality.

For months I felt in my gut something was wrong with two circumstances in my business life. In both cases, I just did not believe the rhetoric. Deep inside I felt uneasy, about what I was being told, the statistics, the recommendations being made: by a lot of little signs. Things just did not 'add up' to me.

The plans looked unrealistic based on my experience. *'Maybe I am out of touch? Maybe I have become the dinosaur I have always feared I would become?'* I did not believe the scenarios, but those closer to it said I was wrong. I lost confidence in my own view, and lacked the courage to speak up to insist on a different course. I was worried I'd be showed up to be 'yesterday's man'.

So I left it. As things further deteriorated, my instincts and judgment started a constant whispering in my ear. I still ignored them, and began to secretly pray for the best.

Problem is, *hope* is not a plan.

I needed to face reality. I needed to trust my instincts. To back my judgment. I needed to TAKE ACTION.

A leader is someone who knows what needs to be done, and then has the courage to get on and do it. I have failed a major test of leadership these past few months. I did not 'show up' when I needed to.

Let me be clear. I blame no-one except myself. It has been my responsibility, and I failed.

I let myself down. And let down others. I am really disappointed with myself for it. Never again. Never again.

Trust your instincts. Back your judgment. Face reality. Have courage. Take action.

It's what leadership is all about.

2.4 D
TO QUIT OR NOT TO QUIT? HERE'S THE ANSWER

Here's an insight about failure. It's a bit controversial. Some will love it; others, like me when I first saw it, might reject it out of hand. With time, it grows on you. I now like it a lot.

Business is changing so fast we don't have time to stick with mistakes. We have to trust our judgment, keep facing reality, trying new things. We must put our energies behind what is delivering returns, for our employers, clients, careers. It's not an easy path to follow. It requires discipline.

That's why I grew to love the quote from the crusty old Brigadier in Evelyn Waugh's *The Sword of Honour Trilogy*, who said this about the first rule of attack. It is a startling insight for each of us, every day.

Never reinforce failure.

Says the Brigadier: '*... don't get mixed up with asses getting in a mess – the best help you can give is to go straight on biffing the enemy where it hurts him the most'*.

When I read that, I paused and thought hard about what this meant, and what I could take from it.

I have always believed in 'never quitting'. It was the family motto of the Kennedys. Walt Disney famously said: *'The difference between winning and losing is most often simply not quitting'*. Persistence is more powerful than brilliance, and all that jazz.

I realised as I reflected on the *'Never reinforce failure'* counsel, I sometimes go a step too far: in trying to sell an idea to a client they clearly don't like; to keep supporting a leadership team that is consistently missing its targets; or persisting with a strategy that is not delivering returns fast enough. Or with a relationship that is just not responding.

Don't.

Think about where you are putting your energies. Are you getting the right returns? Where are you reinforcing failure? Is it time to stop?

Would it be better to spend that time and energy on stuff that IS working and IS delivering – to accelerate progress on the good stuff rather than waste more time, emotion and money on the bad?

I haven't yet nailed how to interpret the crusty Brigadier's advice. It needs to be balanced with ensuring we don't quit where we should not quit, and we do keep persisting where we need to.

Reinforce success where you ARE winning.

It kind of makes sense. I am giving it a go. How about you?

2.5
SET THE EXAMPLE

2.5 A
WHY APRICOTS ARE THE SECRET TO OUTSTANDING LEADERSHIP

To get the best out of teams, leaders have to get one habit right. It's a secret to outstanding leadership, whether you lead a team of three, or 3,000. These two stories are beauties and illustrate the 'habit' perfectly.

The first is about the chief executive of the Australian operations of a global software giant with whom I worked in the mid-90s. His background was sales, where his prowess had seen him rise to the top of a demanding, high-performance organisation.

I asked how he kept his sales team performing, year in and year out. *'The secret is simply this,'* he replied.

You have to be on your own game first – lead by example.

This is what he did. Every year he'd go home to New Zealand. He'd buy several crates of apricots from the local markets, and pack them in the back of his mother's station wagon. He'd then drive to a random suburb, park at the end of a long street, walk along it, and knock on each door to try to sell trays of apricots. *'I challenge myself to keep working on my sales pitch so I had sold the boot load before dark,'* he told me. *'I do this annually to get back in touch with basic selling skills, to prove to myself I can still sell, and then to use that confidence to bring new energy and sharpness to the example I set for our sales teams.'* Outstanding!

Phil Waugh is a former Australian Wallabies rugby team member and New South Wales Waratahs captain. *'How do you week in and week out, game after game, season after season, manage to keep inspiring, motivating and leading your team?',* I asked him.

His answer followed the same theme: you have to set the example.

'If you want your forwards to get to the ball first, you get there first. If you want them to tackle harder, be the hardest tackler on the field. Be on your game. Lead by example.'

Stephen Covey's *7 Habits of Highly Effective People* encourages us to *'sharpen the saw':* to keep improving and fine-tuning our skills. Another rugby giant, New Zealander Brad Thorn, sums it up with this motto, learnt from his father: *'Champions do extra'.*

To be an outstanding leader, get into the habit of being on your game. Lead by example. Bring your 'A game' every day. We can't expect others to behave in ways we want them to unless we're doing it ourselves. Show your teams you never rest on your laurels; that you work relentlessly to *'sharpen the saw'.*

Oh – and eat fruit: it's meant to be good for you!

2.5 B
THE MOUSE, THE MAZE AND THE CHEESE

I can be an impatient person. It's a flaw in my leadership abilities. To be a great leader, you sometimes have to let the pace slow, even if it drives you mad. This story explains why.

Bruce Matchett is the most inspiring, passionate and energetic guy I know. One night in Singapore he told a story about leadership which was a ripper. It made me realise how my impatience made me a less effective leader, and a poor coach. It's stuck with me ever since, and is often front of mind as I counsel colleagues on a course of action. In fact, it helps me shut up.

'I've been working in this industry for a long time, and been a leader for most of it,' Bruce told me. *'There's seldom a problem or an issue the younger team bring to me I have not seen before, and don't know how to fix.'*

'It's like a mouse in a maze. If he's been there many times before, he knows where the cheese is. Rather than go all the way around the maze to get to the cheese, he simply jumps the hedges.'

'I do that. I often know the answer when I see my teams working on an issue. I'm in a hurry. So I jump the hedges to the cheese, and tell it to them. To be a great leader, sometimes you have to let the younger guys find the cheese themselves, even if it slows you down. It is the only way they will learn and grow.'

Let the younger mice find the cheese themselves, even if it slows you down.

My brother Greg is a successful recruitment industry leader. He told a similar story in a speech on leadership to a high performers conference.

'In my youth I was an outstanding kicker of a rugby ball. I could kick a penalty goal from just about anywhere on the field, within reason – even from my own 40-metre line. I was quite simply a brilliant goal kicker.' (My brother does talk like this, by the way, often, and sometimes he's almost telling the truth – sometimes.)

'Years later my elder son was playing rugby and wanted to be a goal kicker. I took him to the park to show him how to do it. I placed the ball. Took five careful steps back, ran in with ease, and kapow ... over the goal posts it sailed. "See, that's how you do it. Place the ball at this angle. Walk back to a comfortable length. Then watch the ball, not the posts. Here, I'll show you again".' And he went on to kick a dozen balls perfectly.

After about 15 minutes his son looked up at him: *'Dad, would it be okay if I had a go?'*

The best way your team will learn is by doing it themselves. Provide a compass point, of course. Then give them the time and permission to work it out, even if there are false starts along the way.

There are always exceptions – when the stakes are too high, or a deadline too pressing. In many cases, it's just about managing your own impatience. Allowing your people to navigate the maze.

I am told the cheese tastes better too when they find it themselves!

2.5 C
AVOID THIS FATAL MISTAKE –
DO IT ONCE AND LOSE FOREVER

I was quite shattered last week when someone did something that appalled me. I was dismayed. Stunned. It hurt me personally, but hurt them much more. This person made one of the biggest mistakes we can make in life. Avoid it at all costs.

Australian business icon David Gonski once said to me: *'Staying pissed off is a luxury in business'.* I have had to remind myself of this these past few days. Happily, I am now reconciled. I realise the person who outraged me actually hurt himself far more than anyone else.

This person broke the most fundamental rule to building a career, and a life to be proud of. Fail this rule, and you will not be remembered well. To succeed, this must be the basis of everything you do.

Be true to your word.

If you make an agreement, shake hands on a deal, or make a promise, then stick to it. Integrity is honouring your word. It does not need to be a signed contract. It's about *your* word.

This person, despite looking me in the eye a week prior and, hand on heart telling me our agreement was on track, knew it was not. He was not going to honour three handshakes confirming we had a firm agreement. He'd been working on another deal for weeks, while keeping me 'warm'. I could accept his having second thoughts and bringing our discussion to a halt. But to keep reassuring of his positive intent while using our deal as leverage for a higher price with another party, now that sucks! I absolutely reject his outright deception and lack of integrity.

I read a business magazine in my Singapore hotel some time ago – an article on the 'Best advice I was ever given', with 20 global business leaders giving their view. One said this: *'The best advice I was ever given was from my Dad, who said: "Your reputation is your most important asset".'*

This person's reputation as being 'trustworthy' was not good when I started dealing with him. I stupidly put that aside. Now his true character was exposed. For the rest of our time, whenever his name is mentioned, we will shake our heads and mutter: *'Oh well, he was not made of the right stuff'*. His reputation with us is gone forever.

His colleagues are sadly tainted by it too. As George Washington said: *'Associate with good men (and women) of quality if you esteem your own reputation: for it is better to be alone than in bad company'*.

Character underpins reputation. It takes someone to really let themselves down like this to get the reminder – the slap in the face. I feel sad for the person involved. And damned passionate about ensuring I never forget my word is my bond. I wanted to give you a little reminder too.

I read this from Buddha: *'Sometimes not getting something you really want is a wonderful present'*. That's how I feel today about that deal. How lucky am I. I did not get what I wanted!

It has also made me feel better to write about it. That's because I am small minded and weak – but heck, I do feel better.

2.5 D
HOW TO WIN WITHOUT TRYING TO WIN

I was in the midst of my most terrifying role: coach of an under-10 fourth-grade rugby team. It taught me big lessons about life, business and success.

When I reluctantly agreed to coach the under-10 fourths rugby team, I dusted off notes taken when world record undefeated Brisbane Roar soccer coach Ange Postecoglou spoke to our leaders.

Therein was the insight I used (with co-coach John) to help this team build confidence, improve and have fun.

Focus on the way you play, not on the scoreboard.

This is how Ange coached The Roar to a world record number of games undefeated (of any sport). *'I forgot totally about winning or losing. Instead, I focused energies on playing the game the way we trained, and to play to our key indicators. Sometimes we'd win 1-0 and I'd be unhappy as we'd not played to our game plan. Or, in the early days, we'd lose 0-2 but I would be thrilled, because we were making progress on our game plan. Eventually we improved, and consistently delivered a winning style of play.'*

With Ange's voice ringing in my ears, I told the boys at the first training session: *'Here's our plan: we are going to be the best team in the competition at four things: tackling, attack, passing and spreading in defence. It's all we are going to focus on. Every week our goal is to see a 10% improvement in how we play to our plan. We don't care about the scoreboard'.* They looked at me blankly.

We lost the first four games, but kept true and made progress against our plan. Then we started winning. At each half time, and at the end of games, we reviewed how our plan was being delivered. The boys knew what was expected, and were keen to be judged on how they were doing against the plan. Oh – and they told me they were having *'heaps of fun'.* The *culture* was building.

James Kerr writes in *Legacy*, a book on what underpins the unrivalled success of dominant rugby team the All Blacks: *'Collective character is vital to success. Focus on getting the culture right: the results will follow'.*

If you want to succeed, focus on the way you play, not on the scoreboard.

If you have the right plan, set the example, and keep improving on the way you execute, success will come. Keep that plan simple. Also, be a realist. If the plan is not delivering results, then change it. In the words of comedian Andrew Denton on how he stayed at the top of stand-up comedy for so long: *'When in doubt, change the routine!'*

Postscript

The under-10 team got to the grand final, where they were well beaten by a better team. What a season! What fun! Will never forget it. Big thanks to co-coach John, who actually knew what he was doing!

2.5 E
A FATAL GAP IN MODERN LEADERSHIP –
AND HOW TO FIX IT

I thrive on pressure. It's a strength. And a weakness. So I was delighted when the toughest guy in the world (no kidding) told me he loves it too. It's a solution to ineffective leadership.

Explorer Tim Jarvis told the story of his retracing the extraordinary 1916 expedition by Ernest Shackleton and five companions. Tim repeated their incredible journey, sailing a small rowing boat with five others 800 miles through the roughest ocean in the world, from Antarctica to the island of South Georgia.

He said the teamwork and motivation of the crew was outstanding when they were under pressure on the high seas. But as soon as they landed on solid ground, and rested, discontent, disagreement and disunity began to unfold. People began to think about themselves more than the team. His message is simple:

Pressure builds teamwork.

At Singleton Ogilvy & Mather in the early 2000s, the motivation was clear. It was said a bullet was fired at your head the moment you joined: your challenge was to run as fast as you could to stop it hitting you.

It was, simply put, a high-expectation environment: a tough, uncompromising place. Very hard-working. There was a compelling purpose, high expectations and clear goals. All about the client and results. They say *'purpose-driven organisations'* have the best chance of success. Well, the purpose was clear and unapologetic – DELIVER RESULTS.

Some hated it. They usually left quickly. Fair enough. The people I respected there absolutely thrived on it. It was a badge of honour to survive and make it in that agency. They said if you could make it there, you could make it anywhere. And dammit – it was true.

A pillar of that culture was the Monday 8.30am meeting. Every person in the agency had to turn up. Agency CEO Chris Mort led the session. These were tough guys. Anyone could be called on to update on something. Hearts beat fast. Adrenalin flowed. It was frightening, wonderful and totally inspiring.

I have always found the most motivated, happiest teams are those with 10% too much work to do.

No doubt that's a seriously out-of-fashion view. So be it. Yes it IS all about people: helping them learn and grow, to achieve potential. It's about motivation and inspiration. And, in my experience, the right level of consistent pressure helps deliver that.

Creating a winning culture is about having a clear vision of success, setting high standards, insisting they are adhered to, working with pace and deadlines, communication, and a fair dose of friendly pressure. Take care of the team along the way. Make sure you lead from the front and set the example. Make it a place where team members feel they are special to be part of that high-performing team. Because, you know what? They are!

Of course I have got it wrong. I've pushed too hard, asked for too much, demanded and ranted, and been an insensitive jerk. I continue to learn as a leader, to make mistakes, and try hard to improve.

Bottom line, I have still seen nothing that builds teamwork and a sense of pride faster than being part of a hardworking, high-expectation team, driving real results. It's addictive. Time for me to have a cup of tea and a lie down. Thank you.

2.5 F
THE VERY BEST JOB PERK OF ALL – DO YOU HAVE IT?

I was reading a Facebook staff booklet when I saw something that inspired. It endorses everything I believe about leading high-performance teams. It's a habit Facebook embraces, and one that underpins excellence. This approach will make your team a winner.

Facebook and Manchester United's legendary manager Alex Ferguson have one thing very much in common.

Sir Alex would focus less on teaching technical skills, and more on inspiring players to strive to do better, and to never give up. He recruited what he calls *'bad losers'* and demanded they work extremely hard. This attitude became contagious. Players didn't accept teammates not giving it their all. The biggest stars were no exception. Facebook's mantra is similar, and hugely inspiring.

High standards are a job perk.

If you are serious about your career, then you want to be working alongside winners – the very best. We want to be inspired to push ourselves as far as our abilities can take us.

Our teams, businesses, partnerships and relationships must be underpinned by a core value of excellence: accepting nothing but the highest standard of service, attitude, integrity, transparency, intent. *'Everything we did was about maintaining the standards we had set as a football club,'* Sir Alex elaborated.

Groucho Marx famously said: *'I would never be a member of a club that would have me as a member'.* Pretty insightful. If we know our standards are low, how can we ever be proud of the team that will have us as a member?

Get your teams together and ask yourself these three questions:

- What are the standards we demand we all set, consistently?

- How are we doing right now in delivering to that level?

- What can we do in the next quarter to step up to a higher level of delivery?

Ask yourself the same questions about Brand You! How are YOU doing at meeting the standards you set for yourself, and how is your track record delivering on them consistently?

Former Australian Army chief David Morrison summed up his approach: *'The standards you set are those you walk past'.*

If you see a lowering of acceptable standards, in client service, courtesy, product quality, in whatever shapes your offer, then by doing nothing about it, you set a new, lower standard.

Do NOT walk past inferior standards you and your team are setting. Face reality. Take action. Lift performance. There is NOTHING more motivating or rewarding than being a legitimate member of a high-standards, winning team. I know. I'm lucky enough to have been part of a few.

2.6
KNOW WHEN TO SHOW UP

2.6 A
A LEADERSHIP TIP NOT FOUND IN MANAGEMENT BOOKS

It's only now – decades later – I realise my father mastered the most powerful habit an effective leader can have. No management book I've read has this insight. I hope it is as valuable to you as it has been to me.

I was on a flight to Shanghai. I put on the headphones, started listening to Bach's *Concerto for Two Violins,* and thought of my late Dad. It was his favourite piece.

My memory of him, while a little blurred now, is underpinned by a warm feeling. I remember Dad 'being around' when I was growing up.

Most importantly, of being there when I needed him most. That's the leadership trait I want to share:

A key to leadership is knowing when to show up.

I wouldn't ask my Dad for help. He just 'showed up' when I needed him. He'd pick me up from school unexpectedly when I was feeling down, or appear at my door while I was doing homework, shoulders slumped because a girlfriend had dumped me. He'd ask me to join him for a walk. Or I'd find his arm slipping around my shoulder just when I needed a hug. He'd ask: *'How are you?'* And I'd tell him everything.

My father knew how to keep me on track. I don't know how he did it, but he knew when to turn up for me. With clients and with teams, knowing when to 'show up' is critical. Here are three ways to do it:

- *Trust your instincts:* 'How's George going?' 'Been a while since ...' 'Why do I have a sense of uneasiness when I see that client logo?' 'Why have I got butterflies in my stomach?' 'I wonder what's happening on ...' When you get that nagging feeling, taste something in your instincts, then it's time to 'show up'. Go smell the air with your teams. Ask questions. Test the temperature. Buy someone a coffee. Have a breakfast. Visit a client.

- *Remind yourself:* I have a cue in my office, a paperclip container with the logo of my first ever client, Bridgestone Tyres. Whenever I look at it, I'm reminded to ask myself: *'Time to show up?'* I think about the people and clients I am responsible for. As I think of each, if I get a nagging feeling, it's time to show up. Find a cue. Use it to check in regularly with your instincts.

- *Listen with your eyes:* Always be on the alert for small signals. People not looking you in the eye. Phone calls not returned. Someone gone a bit 'quiet'. Small errors creeping in. A deadline missed. An invoice not being paid. A very slow response (or no response) to an email. You hear of a client complaint. More than one talented staff member leaves a team. Hmmm. What's cooking? Listen. Like a thief. Then check it out.

I don't know how Dad did it. He just knew. Maybe he trusted his instincts, reminded himself regularly that it was time to, or listened with his eyes. Either way, Dad showed up when I needed him to. It helped keep me on the right path. I am grateful for it.

2.6 B
THE KEY TO A WINNING TEAM WILL BE MUSIC TO YOUR EARS

A chance meeting in Melbourne gave me new insight into how to build winning teams. Here's what happened – and the lesson in it for your business and life. Beware – it might depress you. Or spur you into action.

We arrived at the restaurant. My 11-year-old mate grabbed my arm: *'OMG,'* he enthused, breathlessly. *'LOOK! Look who it is!! It's … it's Archie Thompson! And … (gasp!) … Besart Berisha!'* Two strikers from the Melbourne Victory soccer club.

The entire team was in the private room for a pre-season dinner. We looked in from the door. What an inspiring group of young people – beautifully mannered, dressed, welcoming. The mood in that room was excited, warm, energised, inspired and bonded. I wanted to cut off a slice and take it home.

'Now, that's a winning culture,' I said. *'They will do very well this year.'* I knew this because I did just one very simple thing.

I listened to the music in the room.

The vibe resonated, connected, inspired, empowered, calmed, evoked, felt natural and right. I wanted more of it.

If you are a leader, listen to the music in and from your team. Does it feel right, strong, harmonious and on key? If not, look squarely in the mirror, because YOU are the composer. Others have to conduct your tune or play the chords. If it feels off key, take responsibility. It's YOUR doing. Give your team better music to work with. Or, if necessary, you always have the option to change the players. Look hard in the mirror first, if you've got the integrity and courage to do it.

If you're a team member, and the music feels off key and dysfunctional, then you have a choice. Tell the composer (leader), and push him/her for change, or take the lead – and try to 'conduct' a more positive, inspiring rhythm yourself. Don't follow the prescribed script: improvise and play a better tune. Or, join another band.

Four questions for you. Be absolutely truthful with yourself now:

- Think about your work team – how does the music sound right now from your team or within a client relationship?

- If you are the leader, what can you do to change the music?

- If you are a team member, what is making the sound jar? Is it the conductor, colleagues, or is it you – you just don't like playing trumpet any more? And what can you do about it?

- And then think about the three most important personal relationships in your life. How are they sounding right now? What can you do TODAY to improve the music?

'If music be the food of love, play on', wrote Shakespeare in *Twelfth Night.* Use 'music' as the food for progress. Listen to it. Improvise with it. Change it. Make better music. In everything you do.

Postscript

Melbourne Victory ended up champions, winning the A-League that season.

2.6 C
LISTEN TO THIS – THE MOST POWERFUL TIP FOR BUSINESS SUCCESS

When colleague Dave says these four magical words of advice, I know they are pure gold. Yet I struggle to follow them. If you want to succeed in whatever you do, don't be like me. Listen to Dave.

Management guru Tom Peters says: *'I hate MBA programs but if I was to design my own MBA program it would have two streams: Strategic Listening One and Strategic Listening Two'*. Peters knows being a great listener is the key to being effective, adding value and making a contribution.

I am a sporadic listener. Good with clients. Poor with colleagues – though improving. If I want to keep getting better, I have to follow Dave's big four words of counsel on how to become a great listener.

Shut the f**k up.

It's as simple as that. STOP TALKING, and start listening. BE SILENT. Be patient. Let the other person finish what they are saying. Listen to their words and intent. Stop planning what you are going to say next.

Here are five tips to becoming a better listener. They will help you become a more intuitive and insightful leader, colleague, friend and relative.

- Yes – we know. Shut the f**k up.

- Don't interrupt. (Peters calls it *'the 18-second manager'*, who listens for 18 seconds and then interrupts).

- Maintain eye contact.

- Keep as present as you can – force distraction out of your mind; get interested.

- *'Listen to what is being MEANT, not to what is being said.'* Keep searching for the real message they want to convey – what is being meant by those words.

- When they go silent, ask questions. Delve a step further, clarify, probe for more context. Do this before giving your view.

Dave has helped me with my listening. When we meet, we start with chitchat, then he puts his hands on my shoulders. *'Chris – I want you to focus now. Look in my eyes. Keep present. I need you to listen to me for a few minutes. Then I need your counsel.'* As I listen, sometimes I drift away. *'Focus!'* Dave murmurs. I listen. Then I interrupt. *'Stop!'* says Dave. *'Stay silent. LISTEN!'*

Gradually, I improve. Step by step. Meeting by meeting. I am forcing myself to improve, to go into meetings prepared and ready to listen. It all starts with reminding myself of Dave's inspiring advice. Four big words. *'Shut the f**k up!'*

2.6 D
THE RECRUITER, THE BRIEFCASE
AND A POWERFUL MESSAGE

'I have the perfect candidate for this role', recruiter Peter said. He carefully placed his briefcase on my desk, unlocked the latches, and opened it slowly. I saw something then that has stayed with me ever since. It seduced me, and still does so 20 years later. This is what he had in that briefcase.

Nothing. He had nothing in it.

Except one CV – of that *'perfect candidate'*. That was the magic of the moment. It made me feel this one CV was absolutely gold. It stood alone. I could not wait to get my hands on it.

Peter made me wait. He'd half pick it up. Then gently place it down in the briefcase again, and tell me more about why the candidate was perfect. Then begin to pick it up ... here it comes! And then place it down. Torture. Eventually, it came, we hired, and the rest is history, as they say. Here's the point. The magic of that moment was simply this:

Presentation counts.

It really, really, really does. Peter Salt does not even recall this meeting. I do – vividly.

The way you present yourself and your offer is a critical ingredient to 'showing up' for yourself: to ensuring you nail the moment, and 'get it right'.

Whatever you do in life and in business, think about how you present. It might be a document, reception area, meeting room, a table for a dinner, your desk, car and, critically, the way you dress.

One of my biggest disappointments in myself is that I have always dressed poorly. I could have done better. My shoes let me down. When I see someone well dressed, I always bow my head in appreciation and respect.

My mentor, colleague and friend from my Hong Kong days in the mid-1980s, Paula Gaber, talked about *'the oracle of the obvious'*. Making something simple and straightforward (advice to clients usually) seem like a brain wave, 'rocket science' insight. This sums up my next point. Take it to heart! Please.

Before you send something to a client, have a meeting, or leave home in the morning, pause a moment and double check. Are you presenting yourself, your work or your agency in the very best possible light? Be critical. Pay attention.

Every one of us does indeed judge a book by its cover. You know it's true. Don't screw up how you present. Presentation sells. Make it work for you.

2.7
BE PARANOID

2.7 A
WHY PUTTING YOURSELF OUT OF BUSINESS IS SMART

The most dangerous threat to businesses and careers is a great last result. It breeds complacency. FATAL! We must relentlessly improve or we will be overtaken and soon fade into obscurity.

Never rest on your laurels. Andy Grove, a former Intel CEO, famously said: *'Only the paranoid survive'*. David Ogilvy talked about *'divine discontent'*. Only too well do I remember the counsel of a colleague in 1988 who said to me: *'Relax, Chris. You'll be fine. There is nothing more paranoid than a PR guy'*. Here's the point:

We are only as good as our NEXT result.

To grow successful, thriving and sustainable careers and businesses, we have to remain 'divinely discontent' and 'paranoid' about our capabilities, edge and competitors. Here are two ways to do it:

1. Putting yourself out of business

Chris Graves, chairman of Ogilvy PR Worldwide, is obsessed with learning. He never stops reading, searching, asking questions, exploring. He keeps inventing 'stuff': new ideas, thinking, products, methodologies. He is a rare breed, always with an insightful point of view about the future.

When I worked with him in the mid-2000s, he'd encourage us to workshop a session he called 'Putting yourself out of business'. This is how it works.

Pretend you're your own fiercest competitor, or a new hot shop just opened and with big ambitions. The 'pretend' agency's goal is to put your real firm out of business. Brainstorm for an hour about all the things you'd do as that pretend agency to damage and weaken your business.

They'd be sharp ideas, because you know your biggest weaknesses and vulnerabilities. Make a long list of all these actions. Identify the five most dangerous actions this competitor could actually take to hurt you the most.

Develop a 100-day plan to safeguard and protect, deal with or solve those vulnerabilities. Meet every 10 days to monitor progress. Lift your business to the next level of power, momentum and competitive edge. Do it every 100 days. Make yourself bulletproof.

2. Learn from the best

Look at the best player in your category/sector, the competitor you admire and fear the most. What do they have? What do they do? How do they do it? (Maybe it's not a competitor, just another business you really admire.) Then look at your business. What do you do well? What could you do better? How do you move from better to best? What are the five actions you could take from this exercise to lift your business or career to the next level of competitive edge and excellence? Develop the plan. Set deadlines. Get on with it. Monitor progress regularly.

Remain 'divinely discontent'. Never rest on your laurels. Never become complacent. Andy Grove again: *'Success breeds complacency, complacency breeds failure'*.

We are only as good as our NEXT results: only the paranoid survive!

2.7 B
THE JUST-INVENTED FOUR–LETTER WORD THAT WILL SAVE YOU

Edward de Bono sat on stage at the Cannes Creativity Festival and took us through a brilliant stream of consciousness. Then he introduced us to Ebne. I grabbed it immediately and have used it to strive for higher performance. It can work for you. Here is what Ebne is all about.

There has been more change in the past five years than the previous 50. Here's the frightening bit: change will never be this slow again. To survive, we have to embrace de Bono's brand new four-letter word. Without it, our careers and businesses will fade away. I now use it 10 times a day: at work, when coaching myself, even with my children.

It's a word that captures an attitude that is critical if we are to keep ahead of and thrive through the waves of change happening in business, and in our lives.

Ebne – excellent, but not enough.

De Bono: *'I invented this new word because there is a real need for such a word. If you want to change something you have to attack it. We do not have an easy way of saying something is excellent but not enough'.*

So, how to apply Ebne? Here are some examples of how I do it.

I see a good growth plan from one of our businesses. *'That's Ebne,'* I tell the leaders. *'Excellent, but not enough. We have to find that extra 15% of thinking, ideas, innovation and edge to ensure we stay one step ahead. Let's brainstorm, find it and build it into the plan.'* The agenda for our annual kick-off leadership meeting takes shape. We review it. It's pretty damned good. *'But it's Ebne,'* one of my colleagues asserts. *'We need that extra 15% ... that WOW factor to make it a meeting that inspires change and accelerates growth.'* We brainstorm. Do more work. Lift it by 15%.

I give a presentation to a client. They like it. Agree to the proposal. In the elevator I scold myself: *'Ebne, Chris. Yes – it did the job just fine.*

But where was that extra idea or insight that surprised and delighted the client, and gave them unexpected and useful new value?' I meet the team. We brainstorm. Call the client: *'Thanks for the meeting, Bob. One idea I forgot to mention ...'*

Ebne.

Excellent, but not enough. A new word for a new time. Embrace it. Make it part of your business and your attitude. It will help ensure you and your business are the best you can be.

2.7 C
FIJI, THE FUTURIST AND A FRICKING BIG 'SURVIVAL' WAKE-UP CALL

I went to Fiji to speak at a big conference. Flew in late on Thursday, spoke first up Friday, and then flew home. The organisers sent me some notes of the conference highlights. A futurist who did the opening keynote said something brilliant, a startling truth about business today, and a key to survival. Here it is.

We have to be relentlessly dissatisfied about our competitive position if we are to stay relevant. It's about maintaining a healthy level of paranoia, and using that to sensibly adapt and change.

Futurist Mike Walsh, CEO of innovation research agency Tomorrow, crystallises this thought quite handily when he tells us what to do about 'change' if our businesses are to survive. Six words. Energising words. They are in my mind every day when working on growth ideas.

Think new. Think big. Think quick.

Think about your business. Is it obsessed with developing new products and services that your clients need and will buy today and tomorrow? Are these big, game-changing ideas where the nature of what you do evolves to secure a valuable and sustainable future? Are you moving fast enough? Is there real urgency and intent to drive that change with pace?

We have to be genuinely obsessed about delivering today (what's now), and have an absolute focus on tomorrow (what's next). Every company, every year, needs to generate at least 10% of revenues from new services; services that did not exist in their portfolio the year before. For digital businesses, it's more like 30%.

So, what's the biggest barrier to change?

Quite simply, a great last result. *'Hey – things are fine. We're good.'* Bullshit. I read this comment about the need to digitalise in all industries by Rohan Lund, the then chief operating officer at Seven West Media: *'The glory days are the biggest enemy, not digital'.* He's right. Nothing is more dangerous to survival than a great last result. It makes us lethargic and complacent.

So, think new. Think big. Think quick.

Set an hour aside with colleagues. Think hard about your business and growth strategy. Are you thinking NEW? Are you thinking BIG? Are you thinking QUICK? Come out of it with a roadmap of the changes you need to make. Start that journey. There is no time to lose and no second chances.

Postscript

I was in Rome in June. It was stiflingly hot. The street corner vendor sold ice-cream, cold water and the craze of the day: laser pointers. I was back for Christmas. Freezing. There was that same street corner vendor. Selling hot chestnuts, hot chocolate and the craze of the day: selfie sticks. Not exactly earth shattering stuff. Still, it underpins the message: adapt and change. And whatever your worlds: *Think new. Think big. Think quick.*

2.7 D
THE MOST DANGEROUS CLICHÉ IN BUSINESS AND IN LIFE

Tim came to see me looking for opportunity. *'The most ridiculous belief in business is "if you build it, they will come". It's absolute crap'*. I had not thought of that. I liked what he said. It made me think about other expressions we use glibly but are in fact dangerously wrong.

Iconic Soccer coach Ange Postecoglou suggests a beauty: *'If it ain't broke, don't fix it'.*

It's *'the slogan of the complacent, the arrogant or the scared'.* It is without doubt the most dangerous cliché in business. I often fall victim to its seductive smile. Are you a victim too? If so, get ready for failure.

Rather, says Ange, the cliché should read:

If it ain't broke, FIX IT!

His point: when you are on top of your game, change your game.

Things seem fine. Business is on track. The numbers are coming in. You're wanted and needed. Your phone is ringing and people want you involved. You're feeling comfortable.

Now is the time to take action, and to drive change. Here are four habits to help:

- *Only the paranoid survive:* There's nothing more paranoid than a PR guy, right? I am constantly thinking worst-case scenarios, questioning the next step, fretting about the future. It's the first rule of crisis management: plan for the situation to get worse. When things are going really well, I start getting butterflies. David Niven used the expression in his life: *'When the garden is in full bloom – watch out! That's when the weeds are quietly growing'.*

- *Embrace Ebne:* Edward De Bono's invented word for our age is Ebne – excellent, but not enough. Whatever you have going right – analyse it. How can you make it better? How can you improve, get more competitive, sharper, more effective?

- *Action beats reaction:* We had a business in a smaller city. I was told its future was dim. But results improved! It had won work. I put the issue out of my mind. The business suddenly lost two clients and went bad. We closed it. It hurt us. We reacted fast and efficiently. But if we'd taken action earlier, we could have exited with far less pain. Take action proactively.

- *Skate to where the puck is going to be:* Ice Hockey legend Wayne Gretzky, when asked why he was such a good player, responded: *'Because I skate to where the puck is going to be'.* Keep thinking about what is going to be needed in the future: a year away, three years. Start innovating and evolving now so you are ready to be 'in the right place at the right time'. Make sure you're travelling towards where you need to be to exploit opportunities.

I am as complacent as the next and have so many things 'going a bit wrong' that I tremble when asked to also get paranoid about the things going right! I won't overreact. But I will give it thought.

Beware of what Ange called *'the slogan of the complacent, the arrogant or the scared'!* Action beats reaction. If it ain't broke – **fix it!**

2.7 E
LOOK IN THE MIRROR –
CAN YOU SEE THIS TERMINAL FLAW?

We were celebrating our client's triumph in the most hostile takeover in Australian corporate history. Then its chief executive sobered the mood with a warning that has stayed with me ever since. It is a massive 'watch out' for businesses and ourselves.

When Campbell Soup Company launched a takeover bid for Australian biscuit maker Arnott's in 1991, the newspaper headline screamed: *'US cookie monster wants to gobble our Arnott's'*. So began a hugely emotive and aggressively fought takeover war. It ended with Campbell gaining control at the last gasp, against all expectations.

The celebration cocktail party was in full swing a few weeks later. Then Campbell CEO David Johnson gave us this chilling warning during his speech. *'Enjoy the moment,'* he said, *'but remember this ...'*

Today a peacock, tomorrow a feather duster.

I was reminded of it when a colleague shared a great David Ogilvy saying: *'Don't be so easily happy with yourself'*.

Just about the most dangerous trait in business is when someone starts showing 'hubris', defined as: *'Extreme pride or arrogance, often indicating a loss of contact with reality and an over-estimation of one's own competence, capabilities and accomplishments, especially when the person exhibiting it is in a position of power'*.

I've seen 'hubris' in big CEOs, in politicians, among colleagues and competitors. Every now and then, I've seen myself flirting with it. STOP! Look hard in that mirror, often, and when you see a touch of hubris winking back at you, take action. Get it under control. Fast.

It's fair to build self-esteem and confidence by rationally and relevantly acknowledging our achievements. Be on the alert, though.

Whenever a sense of self-satisfaction starts creeping in, it's time to dust off Johnson's words. Remember:

- It takes very little for our position of strength to be eroded or taken away.

- Take nothing for granted.

- Keep absolutely focused on what you can contribute next.

- We are only as good as our next result.

- Remain paranoid, always (nothing is more dangerous than yesterday's success).

- Never rest on your laurels.

- Keep relentlessly dissatisfied with your own performance and contribution.

It's the approach that has driven the success of the All Blacks, the world's most successful sporting side ever. The Maori have a word for it: *mana*. It captures all the qualities of great personal prestige and character, built around humility. Leaders with mana understand the strength of humility. It's the foundation of character.

Today a peacock, tomorrow a feather duster. Keep it with you, always.

2.8
EMBRACE CHANGE

2.8 A
WHY SOME ENTREPRENEURS SUCCEED, AND OTHERS DON'T

I have been in Asia meeting with independent agencies – businesses built by hard-core entrepreneurs. Every conversation proved it is one simple ingredient that ensures success or failure. We need to learn this lesson.

Each of the 150 or so companies I met started life with an idea, and with courage. We could quickly see which were 'future ready' and fit for the next five years. Many were on the cusp of a death spiral. They could not see it. We could. They were stuck in the present, and had not embraced one thing critical to survival in business.

Actually, I knew the secret before I went travelling to identify partners for our Asian growth plans. Entrepreneur David Tudehope had shared it over a hurried lunch in Sydney a week prior. David founded Macquarie Telecom and built it into a major and resilient force in the Australian telecommunications market.

'David,' I asked, *'what has been the secret to your success?'* His answer has been front of mind as we've assessed potential partners in Asia.

It's the ability to adapt and change that underpins success.

I knew he was right. I hate change. I like predictability, for things to stay the same. I find change really, really hard. I have learnt change is inevitable. In fact, a thirst for change can give you an inspiring and exciting view on life.

It's not the strongest of the species or the fastest that survives, nor the most intelligent, but those who are most able to adapt and embrace change. Well – Darwin said something like that, and I get it now. Doug Smollan believes: *'Change is our friend'.*

So, how do we get 'change' front and centre in our businesses?

Start by creating a genuine culture of innovation in your company. Peter Williams, an innovation guru, suggests the following as the foundations of innovation:

- Make it part of the strategy.

- Be clear about what you're trying to create.

- Ask for ideas (innovation is about trying new ideas).

- Make it widespread in your company.

- Support it with a funding model.

- Mandate it and measure it (include 'what are you doing that's new?' as a KPI).

- Communicate, communicate, communicate.

And his number one driver of innovation? *'Progress: make small bits of progress.'*

After all, life without change is a life without development, new challenges and experiences. Not an original thought. I stole it. For a change.

Postscript

Here's some counsel on being resilient through change. Arianna Huffington, in her book *Thrive*, references a University of Chicago study about what happened to employees of a big company going through a massive restructure and change. Those who make the transition a success had an attitude summed up in the three Cs:

- *Commitment:* They joined in and tried to be part of the solution.

- *Control:* They had a sense of resolve rather than resignation.

- *Challenge:* They found ways to use the crisis to strengthen themselves, to build resilience and grow.

2.8 B
ARE YOU DEALING WITH CHANGE FAST ENOUGH?

I was listening to Blondie while running the streets of Jakarta (not an easy task, let me tell you: me running, and running in Jakarta!). I reflected on what an extraordinary talent Debbie Harry has been. How had she stayed relevant for so long? The internet gave me the answer.

Debbie Harry puts it this way:

You must be constantly reinventing to stay on top.

Fair enough. But how do you do it and what are the risks? Brands that have failed or are failing, according to *Collective* magazine, have two problems in common:

- *Preservation obsession:* They are unwilling to change as times and needs evolve; traditions become an anchor that holds them back when they should be a foundation on which to build the future

- *Progress addiction:* It is equally dangerous to change too much too quickly, or to simply make changes for the sake of it.

So how can we best learn to *'constantly reinvent to stay on top?'*

First, we need to be regularly challenging ourselves around 'change'. Avoid 'preservation obsession' and, just as importantly, avoid 'progress addiction'. We also have to change while delivering the right returns today.

Keep thinking hard about the change you and your business need to deliver to clients, today and tomorrow. Be outstanding in trying to predict client needs. Do not think clients know what they need. As Henry Ford said: *'If I'd asked people what they wanted they would have told me a faster horse'.*

Read constantly. Keep track of what the thought leaders are saying at the big bleeding edge conferences within your specialty around the world. Read the trade press. Read the blogs and websites of the very best in your industry. Learn from the major companies and their market announcements.

Ask yourselves: *'How do we need to – sensibly, commercially, cleverly – evolve and change to remain vitally relevant and indispensable to our clients, while making a relevant return for our shareholders along the way?'*

Get the balance right between preservation obsession and progress addiction. Remember – change is not an event: it is a process.

2.8 C
WHY TAKING THE EXIT DOOR SAVES YOU

It was 3am in my hotel room in New York. The fire alarm shattered the silence. What happened next sums up why so many fail to survive life-threatening crises, or to survive the change under way in business.

I thought the alarm would stop. It didn't. Everyone on our floor headed out into the corridor, pyjama-clad, dazed and scared. Someone screamed. I smelt smoke. The fire escape beckoned. I stopped. I did not want to go through that door. That hesitation sums up why so many fail to adapt to the massive transformation taking place in business. It's summed up in an expression I heard last week.

Progress always involves risks. You can't steal second base and keep your foot on first.

I read that people won't take the 'exit' option because they do not know where the stairs will take them. This is exactly what I felt in New York that night: *'Where do those stairs go, will they lead me to safety, or will I be trapped with even less chance of escape?'*

Here's perspective from David Cottrell and Robert Nix, taken from their book, *Indispensable*. *'Every time you go through an exit, whether it is job related or personal, you are making an entrance into a new opportunity ... You cannot move forward without having the courage to exit the familiar.'*

To stay a step ahead of change – to disrupt ourselves more than our most disruptive client is disrupting us – we have to have courage. Change is really, really, really hard to do. I think so anyway, because it is for me.

But change can also be awesomely inspiring. To take risk, to push into the uncomfortable: to take your foot off one base when you are prepared to get to the next. To take that exit door when you don't know exactly where it is going to lead. To take a risk and to succeed is to experience, in full, the joy of being alive.

If the rate of change outside an organisation is faster than within, the end is near. Same applies to us: our offers to our employers and clients must keep evolving. We are only as good as our NEXT result! We have to keep changing.

Feel the fear. Embrace it.

Back yourself. Take that bold step through that exit door. Chances are, you'll be fine. Seriously. Keep moving, keep believing, and keep trusting. Remember: it's okay to fail. To fail a little is an inevitable outcome of stretching yourself. It's how you get better. Allow yourself to feel afraid. I'm totally up for it. Are you?

2.8 D
THE NEW BLACK IN CAREER MANAGEMENT

Heed this critical lesson from a young truffle farmer from the Luberon, Provence, if you are to safeguard your career. Ignore it at your peril. Embrace it and thrive.

Farmer Johann was energised as we walked through his olive grove. *'I quit banking to run my 90-year-old grandfather's farm. I am his sole heir, and needed to get involved. It was pretty run down. Some olive trees and vines. I realised my only route to survival was to diversify – to add new revenue streams and offerings that could cater to a wider range of customer and provide protection from seasonal factors beyond our control.*

'I've planted more olives, have a "sponsor an olive tree" program under way, have started farming truffles, have created a "truffle hunting" tourist activity; we have bees for honey, offer wine-crushing experiences, charge a fee for tourists to pick grapes and olives, and will also start fishing tours of the lake and river. It's the only way we keep up with change, and leverage what this place has to offer.'

I listened in awe. Johann's approach was so wise. It struck me that it is exactly what anyone in business today needs to be doing if their careers are to thrive.

Diversify your skill set – or soon perish on the scrapheap of has-beens.

Harsh, but true. Certainly in my industry, and I bet in yours too. Businesses are changing so quickly it's almost impossible to keep up. Marketing, for example, is now less about a series of specialist capabilities, agencies and offerings, but rather a 'rush to the middle'. Lines are blurring. Competition for the same budgets is exploding.

So, what does this mean for careers in this fast-morphing world? You got it. Diversify that skill set.

I'm not suggestion a revolution. Stay calm. What I am saying is this: what got you here won't get you there. You need to keep evolving your knowledge, capability, value proposition. One step at a time.

Just as Johann is continually reading his market, and innovating to add spice to his offer and revenue streams, so must you. Here's how:

- Become addicted to learning. Lap it up. Search it out.

- Read, read, and read. Books, magazines, online, offline, industry trade press, the lot!

- Learn to code – just a little.

- Keep connected to the street – the trends, vibe, language, habits.

- Stay close to technological innovations (talk to teenagers – they'll tell you about stuff you have no idea about).

- Keep a robust point of view alive about the future – about your role, client challenges and the changing channels to customers. It does not matter what it is about, so long as it involves the future, and how your business can add value in that future.

There's no growth in your comfort zone. Step boldly into new learning. Keep a constant eye firmly on the radar of your industry, spotting gaps and opportunity to evolve.

By just having that attitude, you'll already be one step ahead. Diversification will keep that farm in Provence relevant and robust. It will do the same for your career. That's a promise.

2.8 E
IF YOU WANT A GREAT NEXT ROLE, GET ILL FIRST

'It took me 130 coffees to land the ideal next role for me,' said my breakfast companion. 130 coffees, hey. That would make you pretty ill. That's the point. You need to get ill if you are to secure the very best opportunity you can. Here's why.

I am a huge fan of making the grass greener on this side of the fence by evolving your current role to be more rewarding. Sometimes the reality is we need to move on.

As your career evolves and you get more senior, it becomes tougher to 'land' the perfect next role opportunity. That's where the 'Get ill first' strategy comes into play. Here's how it works.

It's all about information, leads, learnings – ILL.

Every coffee meeting provides an opportunity to extract three things:

- *Information:* About your industry, your skill sets, what's happening, the trends, the needs.

- *Leads:* To new people to meet, to opportunity.

- *Learnings:* About potential roles, what skills are in demand, how to shape your offer to best match demand.

'I had 130 coffee meetings. I contacted people who I thought could lead me to others. One coffee introduced me to three more, and so it evolved. About 25 of those meetings ended up being 'important' on the path, and those 25 led me to the five key conversations that led me to that perfect role,' my companion explained.

Leadership coach Rob Irving gave me this insight: *'You need 49 "no's" before you get a "yes". A "no" is not a "NO – you don't win" situation: it's a coffee meeting that does not provide a firm conclusion on your search for, in this instance, a new role'.* It's all about persistence.

These meetings are the key to evolving your career, or building your business, if you approach them with the right mindset. Here's another angle on them.

I'd been CEO of Ogilvy PR for several years, having sold my PR firm into the group. I was stale and wanted a change. I did not have the courage to quit, fearing a life selling bananas on street corners if I left security for the unknown. Then Rob Irving gave me this advice. I quit the next day. This is what he said:

'Don't get fixated about having clarity of what you will do next. Relax – what you do next will become apparent. Have the courage to "make yourself available" to new ideas and opportunity.' Remember the words of author André Gide: *'Man cannot discover new oceans unless he has the courage to lose sight of the shore'.*

Have confidence that the right opportunity will evolve. Have as many conversations as you can. Talk about your passions, and theirs, about their challenges and business issues. Keep an open mind.

Allow yourself the freedom to explore. Have courage that what you do next will become apparent. It will become obvious to you at some point. It might well not be what you expected or could have anticipated. Oh – and it might also involve drinking some coffee along the way!

Postscript

I bumped into a former colleague, Phil. When he had left our group a few years prior, he was anxiously unclear on what to do next. I counselled: *'Relax. What you do next will become apparent'.*

'So, what did you end up doing?' I asked. *'I started a firm with partners. After a while we disbanded the partnership, I rebranded the business and have never looked back. Things are great!'* *'What did you call the new company?'* I asked. *'Oh, you should know. You told me what it would be called,'* he replied. *'Huh? What do you mean?'* *'Well, you said what I did next would become apparent. So, I rebranded that company Apparent. What I did next has indeed become Apparent!'* (http://www.apparent.com.au/)

2.9

BE RELENTLESSLY PERSISTENT

2.9 A
A GOLD MEDAL–WINNING HABIT TO REMEMBER

My mind kept wandering while watching the London Olympics to the greatest Olympic moment ever (for me): a moment of disaster, and triumph. It's a moment with a powerful message for life and success.

When I think about the greatest Olympic champion of all, I think not of Bolt, or Phelps, but of an unknown Australian who achieved gold by believing in one thing:

Do not give up.

He persisted. That's how Steve Bradbury won the 1,000 metre short track speed event at the 2002 Salt Lake City Winter Olympics. With one minute to go, Steve was coming stone last. There was seemingly no chance he'd catch the winners. Did he give up? No. He persisted. Relentlessly. What happened?

All the other contestants crashed and landed on the ice. Bradbury sailed past them and took the gold.

Walt Disney once said: *'The only difference between winning and losing is most often not quitting'.* Persistence. It is a key to achieving goals and making progress.

You will always get setbacks. Persist. *'Perseverance is a great element of success. If you only knock long and loud enough at the gate, you are sure to wake up somebody.'* So wrote Tom Morris in *True Success*. *'We need a stubborn consistency in pursuing our vision, a determined persistence in thought, and action.'*

There will always be barriers. If some rocks cannot be removed, go round them. Just like a stream does. Do not give up. Pick yourself up and keep going.

Just about every achiever says 'persistence' has underpinned their journey. Business leader Russell Tate had this quote framed on his wall. You might know it already. Doesn't matter. Read it every day. I do.

'Nothing in this world can take the place of persistence. Talent will not: nothing is more common than unsuccessful men with talent. Genius will not: unrewarded genius is almost a proverb. Education will not: the world is full of educated derelicts. Persistence and determination alone are omnipotent,' said Calvin Coolidge.

Are you persisting, consistently, to achieve your goals?

Postscript

Steve Bradbury won the gold medal exactly as he expected to. He got through the quarter finals through someone getting disqualified. His strategy for the semis was to follow the leaders and hope someone crashed. They did. He came second. In the final he knew he was not nearly as fast as the others, so he carefully followed, again hoping for a crash. So it came to pass. Gold! 'Doing a Bradbury' is now part of the Australian vernacular, meaning an accidental, unexpected or unusual win.

2.9 B
A KEY TO MAKING PROGRESS –
YET DAMNED HARD TO DO

The soccer World Cup was upon us. While watching a documentary on the fortunes of six superb Manchester United players from the 1990s I was reminded of this insight, shared with me by my colleague Lukas.

'Well, it's time to quote from that movie "The Best Exotic Marigold Hotel", when the son who is trying to restore the old hotel in India says:

Everything will be alright in the end, so if it is not alright, it is not yet the end.

David Beckham was sent off in disgrace in the 1998 World Cup. He received death threats and criticism from all quarters, but rose again as true champions do. Eric Cantona, banned for nine months after kicking a rival fan who racially abused him, rose again to captain United.

It all comes down to this. You will never fail if, every time you get knocked down, you stand up again. Sure, it is better to 'win'. Bang. Done. Thank you ball boys and girls. That's not life. Setbacks are table stakes. It's how you tackle them that counts. As Churchill said: *'If you're going through hell, keep going'.*

There's a 15-year-old girl I know. Things were not going well. She had missed out on term-end recognition when most of her peers were lauded; was not picked for the musical; was selected in the lower sports team unexpectedly; and was just not cracking it in most of her pursuits. Yet she was disciplined. She put in the hard yards.

She was disheartened, her self-esteem and confidence battered. We talked about persistence: about never giving up. I told her about Gandhi, who said: *'Adversity is the mother of progress'.* She did not appear to listen. I forgot about her for a while.

We bumped into each other a week later. *'How are you going?'* I asked. *'Pretty good,'* she smiled.

'Soon after we chatted, I did something I am really proud of. I got a job. Just 10 hours a week at a neighbourhood café. I banked $120 last week. I have been working hard on my sports game – scored a goal last week. The coach was really pleased. And that musical I told you about: I wrote to the director and asked that she consider me if anyone withdrew. She called. There had been a dropout, and I'm in. I did well in my exams by the way – better than ever before. Oh – and I also nominated myself as a candidate for house captain. There are some excellent candidates. I am having a go. I am pleased I put my hand up …'

I looked at her in awe. Now, that's what I call refusing to stay down. Pull yourself up. Take the setbacks, and the lessons they bring. Do not give up on yourself. Remember *'everything will be alright in the end, so if it is not alright, it is not yet the end'.*

'Success is not final, failure is not fatal: it is the courage to continue that counts.' Not sure who said it, but I like it. And as Calvin Coolidge wrote: *'The slogan "press on" has solved and always will solve the problems of the human race.'* Are you pressing on?

Postscript

It's a couple of years since my conversations with that young girl. Guess what? She kept on pressing on. She is just entering her final year at school and has been made a school prefect. *'Everything will be alright in the end, so if it is not alright, it is not yet the end.'*

2.9 C
WHAT THE MEDIA TYCOON TOLD ME
ABOUT BUILDING SUCCESS

I had been losing heart about something I love doing. Then, at breakfast with one of the most powerful media industry leaders in Australia, he said something that gave me the compass point to getting my mojo back.

This leader had agreed to share his thoughts on how to build successful businesses in Indonesia. Wisdom and insights flowed from him. But it was this throwaway line I grabbed and have used to help get something very close to me back on track:

If you want to make progress, you simply have to keep schlepping around.

He explained this Yiddish word – schlepping – meant: *'to keep moving around, to continue a journey or path, sometimes with effort, often reluctantly or laboriously'*. I needed that.

For the past few months, I had been losing heart in my blog, *Possums*. Subscriber levels were not increasing – or at the most, inching upward. Every day I'd get 'ping', another notification or two of people unsubscribing. I was feeling 'spent', struggling to produce content, and it seemed to me that my audience was drifting away. I stopped writing for a while. Then five things happened in a week:

- I was in a hotel lobby in Singapore. A guy walked up. *'Hi, I'm Peter. I worked at Ogilvy PR eight years ago. I am now a senior sales guy at Blah. I read your blog every week. Only yesterday I quoted something you'd written, when I told a colleague "you don't remember what people said, or did, but you always remember how they made you feel".'*

- An hour later, a colleague I had not seen for a year said: *'And I realised she was exactly the sort of person you described in your blog a few weeks ago: some people energise you, others deplete. And she's a depleter.'*

- A senior HR executive emailed to ask whether, having read an idea in a *Possums* post, we had a capability in a certain employee communications area to help her company roll out blah, blah, blah. I saw her in Melbourne shortly after.

- I received an invitation to speak at a conference attended by 100-plus CEOs of the largest foreign-owned companies in Australia – some clients, many juicy prospects. The conference organiser mentioned she is a *Possums* reader and wanted me to cover content she had read in a post.

- Then, an email from a senior businessman. His son was at a talk I gave (based on material developed for *Possums*) last week, and had mentioned his reaction to his Dad. As a result, an invitation to speak in two weeks at this client's annual leadership meeting. Two of our companies already work with them. Two others are pitching big work. Perfect timing.

So, my heart has lifted. I have realised good things come when you '*keep schlepping around*'. Keep going, even if it feels like progress is limited and outcomes marginal for a while.

Good things DO come from it. You ARE making progress, you ARE making a difference.

2.9 D
SOUTH AFRICA'S 'ELVIS' –
A LESSON FOR LIFE AND BUSINESS

'I wonder, how many times you have had sex? And I wonder, do you know who will be next?' Odd question! Who is asking and why is it relevant?

Having grown up in South Africa in the 1970s I know only too well the fame and influence of American folk musician Rodriguez. So the Oscar-winning documentary on his amazing story, *Searching for Sugar Man,* was extra special. (Those lines from his song 'I Wonder' ... quoted above, were intriguing and exciting to a generation of young South Africans brought up in a highly censorial, apartheid South Africa police state.)

The story documents the search for Rodriguez, bigger than Elvis in South Africa but unheard of in his native America. Nothing was written or apparently known about him. He was rumoured to have killed himself. The searchers hit a big obstacle in their search. Most would have given up, but they didn't. Their attitude was this:

An obstacle is an inspiration.

I love that. I know the feeling. Whenever I am told something can't be done, or the way forward is blocked, or someone has built a barrier between me and my goal, I get excited. My heart literally beats faster. I can feel it now doing just that.

For me, an obstacle becomes sport. It becomes a secret bond to myself. *'Of course it can be done. There is a way. We can do this. It will just need a smarter or different approach, and maybe harder work.'*

Former US senator Ted Kennedy says the biggest lesson his Dad taught his four sons was: *'never give up'.*

This begins with how we react to obstacles. Like the journalist interviewed in *Searching for Sugar Man,* see every obstacle as an inspiration. Embrace it as a gift. See the obstacle as a perfect opportunity to learn and grow. And then attack it with gusto, passion, relentlessness and a sense of adventure and humour.

Remember the three Ps, an unbeatable combination for success: patience, persistence, perspiration.

The Rodriguez searchers found him. He was working as a labourer on construction sites in Detroit 40 years after his records were massive hits in South Africa. He had no idea he was an icon there. Watch the documentary for the rest of this beautiful story.

What's the biggest obstacle facing you right now? How are you going to inspire yourself to smash through it?

And apologies for the provocative introduction! It was vaguely relevant to the story. That's my excuse, and I'm sticking to it!

2.9 E
THE SECRET TO SUCCESS – BE WARNED, IT CAN HURT!

The telecommunications executive looked at me expectantly, awaiting my answer to his questions: *'How do I drive my career to "success?"'* I knew the answer, and shared it. He was disappointed. As I knew he would be. Bet you will be too – because it's NOT EASY.

Many of us contemplate what 'success' means – what it looks like for me and how I'll know when I get there. It's one of life's tough challenges, to get clarity on 'what's it all about?'

There is good news though. While nailing what 'success' means for you can be a long journey, the answer on how to get there is right in front of us. Seriously. Achieving 'success' is built around one very simple habit.

The most critical single quality for success is self-discipline.

'Ho hum,' you might well say. *'Is that it? Surely there is more to it than that?'* Truth is, there isn't.

As Elbert Hubbard defines it, self-discipline is the ability to make yourself do what you should do, when you should do it, whether you feel like it or not.

Achieve the success you seek through self-discipline, summarised in these wise words of Brian Tracy: *'Your ability to endure ... to continue taking action step by step, in the direction of your dreams, is what will ultimately ensure your success. If you keep on keepin' on, nothing will stop you.'*

This applies equally to short-term projects: striving for a promotion, winning a major new client, losing 10 kilos, running that marathon. It is all about the small steps along the way.

If you want to achieve your goals and 'succeed' in whatever you are doing, get clear on the outcome, and then focus all your energies on the self-discipline.

Keep on keepin' on. NOTHING will stop you if you do that. Good luck!

Postscript

Just read these wise words from Dale Carnegie: *'Success is getting what you want. Happiness is wanting what you get'*. Food for thought. And I love colleague Andrew's story about his Cypriot Greek father's definition of success: *'Working in air-conditioning and wearing a white-collared shirt'*. Sobering. All of us have a unique perspective on our past, and what we are striving for in our futures. If you're self-disciplined, you WILL get there.

2.10
PLAY WHAT IS IN FRONT OF YOU

2.10 A
THE ZULU, THE RUGBY COACH AND HOW TO KEEP WINNING

I love to be organised: to have a careful plan, clarity on next steps, and then work through those one by one. It's a strength. Increasingly, a dangerous flaw. Being organised a flaw? How can that be?

In the 1964 epic *Zulu*, hordes of Zulu Impis are swarming up the barricades, while a bedraggled group of red-coated English soldiers desperately try to hold them off. Bullets are running short. Soldiers rush back to the ammunition hut. *'More ammo quick!!!'* they scream. *'Fill in the form first,'* says the munitions supervisor.

Madness. If ever there was a time to change agreed procedures, that was it. Robbie Deans, when he took over as coach of the Australian Wallabies rugby team, had a philosophy built around this:

Play what's in front of you.

Yes, have a plan about what you might do when you get the ball in a certain position. But always look up, check out the situation, and *'play what's in front of you'*. Respond to the circumstances.

Here's the lesson for business. We live in turbulent times. The pressure on clients is more intense than ever. Thinking is changing fast, instructions from HQ or offshore shifting goalposts, strategies under fire, tension high.

When you meet with your senior clients, don't expect the last conversation you had with them to still hold true; that they are still focused on what was briefed four weeks ago. Much could have changed.

If you go roaring into that meeting pushing through your month-old agenda, and their mind has shifted to more urgent priorities, your offer will seem irrelevant and outdated.

Rather, start every meeting with questions: *'How are you? What is on your mind? What's your priority right now? Has anything changed since we last met? What are your biggest issues – today?'*

Probe. Explore. Listen. Learn. Then, as the meeting begins, *play what is in front of you.* Calibrate your agenda to be relevant, to address the problems burning in their minds – the issues of NOW.

Play what's in front of you. It will keep you relevant. And keep the rampaging hordes at bay (even if it hasn't always worked for the Wallabies!).

2.10 B
HOW FLIGHT 32 WAS SAVED FROM DISASTER –
AND THE MESSAGE FOR US

Minutes after a Qantas Flight 32 engine exploded, and with the new Airbus A380 on the verge of catastrophe, the pilot suddenly broke all the rules. His mindset shift saved the plane. I wish I'd heard his reasoning and beautiful insight 40 years ago. It would have prevented big anxiety, pain and missed opportunity.

Captain Richard Champion de Crespigny was being interviewed on radio about a charity that helps disabled children learn to ski. *'Hmmmm,'* I mused. *'Wonder what the link is between de Crespigny and disabled children. Why is he the right spokesperson?'*

'Boom, boom went the two explosions,' de Crespigny explained. *'Suddenly, we were experiencing "unconditional engine failure". We immediately followed the process, and worked to identify all malfunctions and aspects of the plane that were not working. The list seemed never ending. Then I changed my mindset, broke the rules and took the first step to saving the plane.*

'Instead of focusing on what we did not have, we instead clarified what we DID have available to us. Once we knew what we had, we could work towards flying the plane to safety.'

Focus on what you DO have, not on what you don't have.

There was the link to the disabled children. Use what you've got to make progress. Stop angsting about what you don't have.

I really like this approach.

It reminded me of my biggest regret in life: allowing self-doubt, shame and low self-esteem to prevent me from taking a risk, having a go, pushing myself forward. I've missed out on many experiences and perhaps greater fulfilment because I always feared somehow I was not good enough.

I recall vividly as a younger man the anxiety and longing, always wishing for something: I wanted bigger, smaller, faster, bolder, thinner, more, less, flashier, a different this and a better that. How great it would be if I had one of those. It would make all the difference. And so on and so forth!

Don't make my mistake. *Focus on what you DO have, not on what you don't have.*

Focus on strengths, the wonderful aspects of our lives, the positive elements we need to be grateful for. In business, focus on what your company does have going for it, and how to leverage those attributes. Don't obsess about the gaps and weaknesses. Same holds true for careers.

It's a mindset for a happier, bolder life. Has to be.

2.10 C
THE BEST IN BUSINESS THRIVE AT THIS ONE TRAIT

It can take intrepid game watchers years to see 'The Big Five' in the African bush. I saw all five in the first three hours I went looking. Buffalo, lion, rhino, elephant, leopard. How could this be? The answer encapsulates what you need to have in your armoury to survive in business today.

Our nine-seater Inyati Game Lodge open-air truck was driven by ranger Piet, with tracker Nelson sitting up front. We left the lodge a couple of hours after having arrived in the bush from Johannesburg. Excitement levels were high. Yet we never expected to see all Big Five within three hours of starting out, given the game reserve was the size of Wales.

Ranger Piet made it happen. He used a mandatory skill needed today to survive and thrive in business. It's all about delivering outstanding results to your customers. Piet knew this. So he adopted one habit to deliver awesome results.

Collaboration.

That's it. Ranger Piet thrives through collaboration. As do the other 15 rangers in that section of the game reserve. They communicate constantly. Even though they work for competing lodges, they know they must work together and share information so their clients have the best experiences possible.

When Piet and Nelson led us to three lions, resting under a tree, they were immediately on the walkie talkie briefing other rangers, with those close agreeing a 'schedule' of who would bring their guests, and when, to view this wonderful sight. They'd then tell Piet about a rhino five miles away, or an elephant just spotted at the waterhole. So the exchange continued.

The end result: delighted customers, having once-in-a-lifetime experiences.

It's the way of the world today. No one organisation or executive can have all the answers or skills to deliver to clients. We have to collaborate: with competitors, specialists, with pirates and nutters, and with whomever can deliver the outcome our clients need.

I like the concept of 'T-shaped executives'. On one level they are highly skilled at what they do and bring. On another they have to be able to collaborate.

There's been much talk about 'change or die' for years now. What rings more true today is 'collaborate or die'. Play what's in front of you. Who do you need to start collaborating with?

2.10 D
THIS IS ABOUT YOU AND IT IS REALLY, REALLY WEIRD

A boss once described me as a 'tricky character' to a supplier. I did not like that descriptor, but with time accepted it. Why? Because it is true, dammit. I was reminded of this when a colleague shared an insight he'd heard at a talk given by a northern English supply chain expert (I was having voluntary root canal work done so could not attend).

It's an old expression I have never paid attention to. Yet it is a critical insight we need to accept if we are to work with and lead people, and manage ourselves. This is what that northern Englishman said about you, and – yip – it's absolutely fair to say about me:

There's nowt queerer than folk.

People are weird. Strange. Complex. Unpredictable. The way they think, react, behave, decide, are motivated, inspired, irritated. The things that delight, infuriate, slight and boost. What's important, and what's not. Every person we deal with has unique weirdness.

We need to recognise and accept people are weird; and you are most likely the weirdest of the lot. I know I am. 'Tricky character' is one of the more gentle things ever said about me. Here are some ideas on how to do it:

Recognise everybody is different: Each will react in their own way to a circumstance. Be alert to that reality when dealing with an individual. Be flexible. Play what's in front of you. Learn to appreciate others and their differences.

Become an outstanding listener: 'Listen to what is being MEANT, not to what is being said.' One of the deepest needs of all people is to be heard and understood. Connection begins with listening.

Put yourself in their shoes: Try to see their reaction and the impact of the discussion from their reality and view of the world: from their perspective. It won't be the same as yours. It makes absolute sense to them, from where they are sitting. They are focused on what they want, not what you want. Their constant thought? *'What's in it for me?'*

Be kind: As the philosopher Philo said, *'Be kind, for everyone you meet is carrying a heavy burden'*. And that includes you, and me. The way we are remembered is the way we treat others. Everyone needs to be understood. We all want our self-esteem nourished. We all desire to be important. When you recognise this, you moderate your response to the other person's behaviour.

Underpinning all of that, accept that you are a bit weird. To others, you are. Keep working to understand why you react and feel the way you do. Manage and control your own weirdness. Make yourself more 'user-friendly'.

I've been lucky with the companies I've owned or led in that we've been able to create what advertising legend Peter Cullinane calls *'the mystical power of we'*: a culture created by diverse individuals who come together as a team at a certain time. Special things happen. Big results are achieved. Lots of fun is had. It does not last forever. It's an elusive 'force' (often those involved try to repeat the magic years later by 'getting the band back together' but it is rarely as good again).

You create 'the mystical power of we' by recognising we're all weird, different, unpredictable, odd. Pay attention to ensuring your weirdness, and theirs, is managed and used for the benefit of all. Remember to honour each person's craving to feel important, and to be appreciated. Is that weird? Probably.

2.11
INSPIRE, INSPIRE, INSPIRE

2.11 A
HOW TO MAKE AN UNFORGETTABLY POSITIVE IMPACT

The furniture tycoon rolled down his car window and told me something that literally changed my world. It also showed what powerful leaders are able to do, and why they are unforgettable when they do it.

We were in the midst of a major house renovation. Workmen, rubble, dust – everywhere. Worse still, big six-figure bills coming in every three weeks. Costs were blowing out. I was losing courage.

It got worse. The architect pushed us to renovate the roof cavity to create more living space. It made sense. But the additional cost was a bridge too far. I could not bring myself to go that extra step.

We had to make a decision by the Monday. We went to the deserted worksite on the Sunday to contemplate. I was confused, petrified, paralysed. Then my neighbour drove up. What he did next summarises my message.

People won't remember what you said, or what you did, but they will always remember how you made them feel.

Paul is an entrepreneur who has built a successful, nationwide high-end furniture business. *'How's it going?'* he asked. *'Not good,'* I sighed. *'We have a dilemma: whether to renovate the roof space. It's the cost. I am so nervous it will be a mistake.'*

'Chris,' he enthused, *'have faith. That extra space is practical, and will add big new value. Do it. You won't look back. Remember – fortune favours the brave!'* And with that he drove off with a wave and thumbs up.

My shoulders lifted. My pulse raced. Optimism built. As Napoleon said: *'Leaders are dealers in hope'.* This self-made man had built a big business by taking prudent risk, by being bold. Of course we should do it! We gave the green light. And have not looked back.

My neighbour gave me confidence: a feeling of hope that inspired me into action. I'll never forget it.

Think about the people who have had the most impact on you (positive or negative). Can you honestly remember all the things they said? Or did? Probably not. But can you remember how they made you feel? I bet you can. Like it was yesterday.

The key to great leadership is the ability to inspire. A good leader inspires people to have confidence in the leader; a great leader inspires people to have confidence in themselves.

If you want to be a genuinely effective leader, learn your own way to inspire and motivate others. I have always been a 'shameless dispenser of enthusiasm'. If you share your sense of passion, you infect and inspire others.

You need to lift people up, to be generous with your energies, and to do it often. After all, it's said our chief want is someone who will inspire us to be what we know we can be.

2.11 B
WHY I TOLD MY WORK COLLEAGUE I LOVED HIM

Shaking the hand of a colleague at a meeting's end, I looked him in the eyes and said: *'Arthur, I love you'*. I meant it. He did not immediately phone the HR department 'hotline' for urgent counsel. Here's why.

I was jogging – listening to, aptly, Meat Loaf. I had an intriguing meeting the next morning with a colleague on the cusp of taking a client-side role. I was not sure how to handle the meeting. It was Mr Loaf who gave me the answer with this protestation:

'I want you, I need you, but there ain't no way I'm ever going to love you ... now, two out of three ain't bad.'

Wrong! Two out of three is not good enough. As a leader, you have the power to influence and inspire others you want the best out of, and the best for. You must also give them the respect of honesty, care and 'love'.

Clients don't care about how much you know until they know about how much you care.

That's a David Ogilvy–ism about clients. It also holds true for how we need to behave with those we work with.

This colleague deserved honesty and transparency. I needed and wanted him to stay. If he left, important clients would be jeopardised. But two out of three wasn't good enough. So I gave him the most sincere counsel I could. I put his best interests before mine.

'I am worried I will have regrets in years to come if I think "why did I not do it"', he said. I explained regrets could apply just as much to not staying where he is. I told him how I had left a role where, had I stayed another 18 months, a takeover event would have delivered me millions of dollars, which I missed out on. *'Do you regret not staying?'*

My response was spontaneous. *'Not at all. Because if I had stayed, I would never have met you.'* I meant it. I don't regret for a moment missing that 'pay day', because what happened since I made that decision 20 years ago has been thrilling and amazing. My point was essentially to 'have faith'. Whatever decision he made could haunt with regret. He needed to trust his instincts and go for it – whatever 'it' was.

I needed and wanted Arthur to stay. More than anything, I wanted Arthur to be happy. When we said farewell, I looked him in the eyes, and, again with spontaneity, said: *'Arthur, I love you'*. It wasn't weird. It was real, human, true. I hope – when he left that meeting – he felt cared for, and safe.

Do not let the pressures of business cloud genuine and positive intent to give others the best chance for happiness. Use courage and integrity when dealing with people, particularly those you have influence over. Be generous in words and deeds whenever you can.

As Buddha said: *'In the end, only three things matter: how much you loved, how gently you lived, and how gracefully you let go of things not meant for you'*.

Do I do it all the time? Of course not! I'm often a grumpy git who bullies and pushes, can be emotional and unreasonable, selfish and self-centred. I want to do better. And Meat Loaf has given me the clue how to do just that.

Are you showing enough 'love' to those around you?

2.11 C
INSPIRE PEAK PERFORMANCE –
A LESSON FROM STEVE LYONS

I am thinking of the moment my dear friend PK and I held our darling former colleague Steve's hands as he passed away in Kuala Lumpur from cancer more than a decade ago. I remember the most inspiring habit Steve had. It defined him. Do you do this? If not, then start now!

You don't remember what someone said, or did, but you always remember how they made you feel. Steve Lyons was an absolute master at making you feel incredible. He made you feel everything and anything was possible. He lifted your spirits, ambition, drive. He made you believe in yourself. All those touched by Steve know exactly what I mean.

Sitting here at an Auckland Airport café, I have absolute clarity about what it was that Steve would do that was so inspiring. Here it is. Steve, quite simply:

Gave us all a fine reputation to live up to.

'Hey, meet Chris. He is the best client service person in our company.' 'Sam, you are the most organised and efficient person I know.' 'Francis, I just love the way you listen to anyone and everyone. You are an awesome listener. World class. Teach me how you do it.' 'Hey everyone – I want to introduce George from our Manila office. George is the best writer I have ever worked with. You can learn from him.'

Steve made these huge claims about young executives on the way up. The impact was massive. Shoulders lifted. Pride swelled. *'WOW! If Steve feels that about me, then I must have some talent. I am going to work really hard at that skill and become brilliant at it. I CAN do it. Steve said I can.'*

He always picked on skills where we had potential. Away we'd go and work hard at it, and – what a coincidence – we'd end up fricking brilliant at whatever Steve had said we were brilliant at. Steve knew inspiration is about seeing the outstanding capacity in others that even they cannot see in themselves.

There's an 11-year-old I know. He is learning the habit of daily homework, focus and discipline. I was on the phone to his grandmother, knowing he was in earshot watching sport on TV. *'The thing about that boy is he is so organised, and a self-starter. I am impressed with the way he sets about doing his homework. We don't even need to tell him to do it.'* A few moments later the call ended. I walked into the dining room. There he sat at the table, TV off. Pencil, rubber, ruler neatly lined up, his spelling revision in front of him, looking up at me, a spark in his eye and a massive, proud grin on his face.

I am tearing up now just thinking about it.

Our darling friend Steve Lyons gave us fine reputations to live up to. He made us feel like kings and queens of the world. It worked then. It works now. Give it a go. Whomever you bestow this gift on will explode with growth, and will always remember how amazing you made them feel.

Love you, Steve. Always did. Always will.

2.11 D
GET LASHINGS OF INSPIRATION –
WHENEVER YOU WANT IT

Something happened to me strolling the streets of Rome. Crumbling grandeur, faded pastels, Vespas aplenty. I sucked it in and then, kapow, it happened. It's the secret to getting inspired.

My creative juices flowed. I felt energised. Anything was possible: I was invincible and my journey had only just begun. It was a rare, special feeling. I wanted more of it. The environment lifted my spirits.

It's not hugely helpful. I don't live in Rome. My life is elsewhere. I need to find inspiration closer to hand whenever I need it. But how? The answer is right here. It's like flicking on a switch. And hey presto, you have it! This is how to approach it:

Inspiration is for amateurs – the rest of us just show up and get to work.

I read this in *Brain Pickings*. Forget Rome. If you really want to get inspired, sit down and get started. Hard work supersedes inspiration.

'Show up, show up, show up, and after a while the muse shows up too.' That's author Isabel Allende. I love that. It reminds me of personal trainer Michelle Bridges' advice. JFDI. Just fucking do it. When you need to do something and don't want to, then JFDI. And just do it for 10 minutes. If at the end of 10 minutes you don't feel like it, then stop.

Once you get started and in the groove, you don't stop. You get inspired. You create, and get it done. It will work for you, and will work for those you want to inspire into action.

I love to be surrounded by tactile, comforting things. My office is filled with old wooden furniture, books, art, ornaments and mementos: stuff that makes me feel safe, calm, at peace. As Picasso said, *'Art washes away from the soul the dust of everyday life'*. That's what my comforting space does.

My best work though has been done on airplanes, in coffee shops, looking at a wall in a second-rate hotel room. I had no distractions. I just got started. Created. And inspiration came. The king of writers of the 20th century, Somerset Maugham, had a room on top of his house in Cap Ferrat with awesome views (it's still there by the way). He'd walk up there every day, open the windows on the view, and then turn his back on it, writing facing the wall, from 8.30am to 12.30pm, six days a week. *'Show up, and after a while the muse shows up too.'*

As Sven Baker told me over breakfast in Auckland: *'Love the problem, design the solution'.* He gets inspired by the problem. The more gnarly it is, the more enthusiastic he becomes about solving it. He doesn't wait for inspiration. He just does what's required.

There is no magic to inspiration. Don't wait a moment for it to emerge. As Leonard Cohen said when asked how you write a great song: *'If I knew where good songs came from, I'd go there more often. It's a mysterious condition. It's much like the life of a Catholic nun. You're married to a mystery'.*

So, if you are looking for inspiration, look no further.

The power is 100% with you. Do not delay. Get started! Remember – hard work supersedes 'inspiration'. Get cracking right now. Show up, show up, show up, and after a while the muse shows up too.

2.12
STOP BEING SO BLOODY BUSY

2.12 A
STOP BEING SO BLOODY BUSY – THE BEST ADVICE EVER

When a global advertising industry leader told me to *'stop being so bloody busy'*, his words had a profound impact, and changed the way I operate.

Miles Young, who went on to become the global CEO of Ogilvy, opened his speech to the regional PR leadership meeting in Cambodia in 2003 with: *'Now, here's my message: please, stop being so bloody busy'.*

It's counsel that has taught me to slow down, and has helped me become a better trusted adviser, leader and friend. Here's how Miles explained his request.

'Each of you has huge value to bring to clients. You are expert, and have much to offer. But you get so busy on "stuff" that you lose touch with the value you can bring. Slow down. Think calmly. Find "no agenda" time to spend with clients; to really listen to their issues, fears and aspirations. Find time to use your knowledge to provide thoughtful counsel and solutions. Leverage what you know. Make human connections.'

There are three ways I have learnt to 'be less busy' so as to deliver more value. Each is invaluable.

I visit my 'Third Place' once a week

A Starbucks concept. We have home. We have work. We also need a third place we can escape to, where we feel 'safe', and can spend quality time 'thinking'.

For me, it's a café in North Sydney. I go there once a week on the way to work. They're just bringing in the milk when I arrive. I read the papers. Then I start thinking about my life, and my work. What am I spending time on? Is it the right priority? What are my Big Rocks for the month ahead? What are the major issues? How best to solve them? Where could I contribute more? Who needs my help? I scribble, draw, make lists, map it all out on a big piece of A3 paper. Two hours later, I have clarity on priorities, and direction. I always leave my Third Place with a spring in my step.

I meet important contacts for breakfast

I try to have at least two breakfasts a week with key contacts. It's a perfect time to have calm, thoughtful and inspiring conversations. It rarely takes more than an hour.

There is never a firm agenda. Just *'Let's catch up for breakfast'*. I only plan one question: *'How are you?'* Then, I listen.

I know my companions enjoy them too. If I don't set one up for a while, they contact me. I'm getting tearful now thinking about some of the profound conversations I have been privileged to share with wonderful people over breakfast. They expose vulnerability. So do I. The bond strengthens. It makes me feel alive.

Fresh air sessions

Former British prime minister Tony Blair and his deputy, Gordon Brown, would go to New York for two days every few months, and walk the streets – talking debating, aligning. Take 'fresh air' sessions regularly with your colleagues. Go somewhere, walk the beach, run together, have meals, talk. Change the routine, pause and get reinvigorated. Find clarity.

Stop being so bloody busy. We all need ammunition in our bag of tricks to keep ourselves at our best for clients and others we care about. I've outlined three ways that work for me. However you slow down to think and connect, do more of it!

2.12 B
GET ATATÜRK'S BINOCULARS FOR AWESOME CAREERS

Turkish leader Mustafa Kemal Atatürk led the defeat of Australian forces at Gallipoli in World War I. It was at the most decisive moment of that battle that he did something we must copy if we want opportunity-filled careers.

Atatürk arrived at Gallipoli soon after Australian forces had started streaming up a key hill, with Turkish troops fleeing in panic. Within moments the Australians would have triumphed and history's course changed forever. Atatürk ordered his men to stop, fix bayonets and drop to the ground. The approaching Australians, anticipating a Turkish charge, also dropped to the ground. In the ensuing lull, reserve Turkish troops arrived, with big machine guns. The battle turned into a massive Australian defeat.

Where's the lesson for our careers?

Atatürk fought Gallipoli's first hours with binoculars, not a sword.

He stood on the high ground, and watched every move of the battle. This helped him make the right decision. It's a big lesson for managing relationships, businesses and, importantly, our own careers.

To thrive, we must find time to sit calmly on higher ground, pick up the binoculars and take a measured view of the entire landscape of our roles, capabilities and opportunities. How to do it? Here are some ideas:

- Diarise a quarterly one-hour meeting for yourself at your Third Place. Spend it thinking about ... you. Just you. (A 'Third Place' is not home, or the office, but another spot where you can be alone and comfortable.) Brand these sessions in your diary as 'Atatürks'.

- In this meeting, review Brand You, the four pillars that make up your personal brand at work:

  a. *Delivering outcomes:* Am I being ruthlessly effective and efficient every day, getting more of the important things done consistently?

b. *Expert in something:* Am I deepening expertise and fame as an 'expert in something', the one thing my colleagues acknowledge I am really good at, and often ask me for advice about?

c. *Point of view:* Am I regularly developing points of view about the future, and using that to build profile as someone who is anticipating change and helping my company be 'future proof'?

d. *Collegial and supportive colleague:* Am I doing enough on key relationships with colleagues, and being known to do the right thing?

- Then ask yourself the question Andrew Denton put to our leaders: *'I survived as a stand-up comic by following this golden rule: when in doubt, change the routine. Are you changing your routine enough?'* Are you stale? Do you need to refresh?

- Then lift the binoculars and look more broadly, and ask this question: *'How do I skate to where the puck is going to be?'* How do our skill sets, capabilities and relationships need to evolve to ensure we are 'the perfect fit' for what will be most in demand in a year or two?

- Finally, look hard at the terrain: How can I stay connected with what is happening 'in the street'? How do I best stay 'current'?

Make sure you are spending regular time, with binoculars in your hands, looking at every aspect of your responsibilities and career: the battle you're engaged in today, how to make a sharper contribution to the 'now', what the future looks like, and how you need to evolve to be perfect for that future.

Have you planned your next 'Atatürk hour' yet?

2.12 C
A PRESENT TO CHANGE YOU FOREVER –
IF YOU PAY ATTENTION

Dave said it to 300 of our staff. Cricket coach Paul told it to the under-11 team. Two stories. One powerful message for business and life. A gift indeed.

Coach Paul: *'Cricket is more than a game. It teaches you lessons in life. Of resilience, courage and, importantly, of focus.'* Dave said it as we trained colleagues in customer service excellence. *'The most critical skill we have is to be great listeners. To do this, we have to master the skill of concentration – to be absolutely present at all times.'*

I can be brilliant at this. And terrible. When on form, I flick an imaginary switch in my back and – kapow! – become totally present for a series of complex meetings. When off my game, I can be in other, Walter Mitty-esque worlds, adding nothing, slowing others down. I titled this post as a present for you, and that present is this:

Keep working, always, on your skills to be PRESENT in everything you do.

In cricket, a batsman's concentration is 100% in the moment – the bowler running in, the field positions, the glare, the likely bounce and pitch. Total focus. The ball is bowled, the shot played … and then … aaaaah … relax, look around, breathe. Then it starts again, absolute focus on the next ball. Nothing else matters. There is no room for daydreaming.

Eighty per cent of the time I am totally 'on'. My ability to stay focused and deep in a topic is excellent. Here's the problem. Twenty per cent of the time I am distracted. Everyone feels it. It's disrespectful. You are a waste of space.

I was in a meeting when I said something that showed I had not been present (I was doing a to-do list while others talked). *'Keep up,'* my colleague growled. That hurt. Because first, it was fair, and second, I am a 'concentration ninja' and had let myself and others down.

Keep working on your powers of concentration and your ability to be absolutely 'present' in every meeting and conversation you have.

It's more than just durability and stamina – though that is part of it. It is about training yourself to become brilliant at concentration. IMF chief Christine Lagarde is famous for all three: durability, stamina, awesome concentration.

'If you notice your mind wondering, simply notice where it went, then gently escort it back to the present moment.' So wrote Arianna Huffington. Sometimes I even say to those I am with: *'I am sorry – my mind drifted. Would you mind repeating the last two sentences? I want to make sure I don't miss a thing'*. Most times they respond with patience, and appreciation. They know it's hard to stay focused, and respect a transparent effort to do just that.

A bit weird no doubt. But it works for me. How about you? How do you help yourself stay present as often as possible?

2.12 D
REPLACE FoMO WITH JoMO –
A SIMPLE TIP FOR A BETTER YOU

I did something this weekend so outrageous I am still in shock. I think it's legal. It sure was difficult to do. I liked it, and I'll do it again. It's a bit embarrassing, though. Want to join me?

Andrew Denton is a comic and creative leader. He wrote about FoMO – Fear of Missing Out – the term given to those addicted to social media, desperate to know the latest update about everyone and everything.

Denton has a twist. He has invented a new word that suggests a different concept altogether. It was a perfect match to what I did at the weekend. His new word?

JoMO – Joy of Missing Out.

Denton believes it is okay to disconnect, to not attend an event, read a paper, or edit emails. It's okay to daydream, to imagine, to 'be', to turn the technology off. There is joy, he says, in missing out. Suck in some JoMO instead of filling pipes with FoMO. It's a better addiction. JoMO will give you power, ideas, clarity, connection.

It resonated. Then personal development coach, Clare, counselled: *'Chris, try this weekend not to write one to-do list, don't work on emails, do not write a blog post, or redraft a chapter of your book. Find time and space to unplan this weekend'*.

I tried it. Laptop stayed off all weekend. I walked around the garden, read a book, sat in silence. I watched *Schindler's List* and *Searching for Sugar Man* on Foxtel on Sunday morning. I haven't watched TV like that for 20 years. Do you know what happened? Not much.

Except, something weird. I had thoughts: indicators, prompts ... about stuff I wanted or needed to do. Feelings, bubbling out of nowhere. Kind of appearing in front of me: *'Oh yes, I must do that. It's time. It will make me happier'*. Clarity. Unplanned.

On Monday I went to the city and bought new clothes. I cannot explain adequately what a HUGE step this was for me.

I called my mother and told her I loved her. And made 11 phone calls to colleagues and clients: all on snippets of unfinished business; most times, me saying 'thanks ...'

Oh, I also called my dealer. He's sending over half a kilo of JoMO. I am going to try some more next weekend. Not sure what it will do to me, except give me pointers on what to do for me next. Unplanned. Can't wait to find out what's in store.

2.12 E
I HAVE BECOME ADDICTED TO THESE MOMENTS – YOU WILL TOO

Something extraordinary happened last week. And the week before. I want more of it. Much more. Are you getting enough of this?

CEO Mike made his world famous snapper pie on Monday. He cooked it in the building's industrial oven and served it to our small HQ team of five. From our hectic realities, we suddenly sat quietly, focused on food, talked and communed. Just for 45 minutes.

Two days later, I received a letter with sad news: the passing in the UK of an aged aunt with whom I'd lost touch. It was written with care and respect by someone I did not know. I re-read the letter a dozen times, felt its tactility, have filed it away.

I know this all sounds obtuse, but it is haunting me. You see, I loved those moments. And want more of them.

Moments of real.

I heard the expression in a training session I ran in Singapore. It has sat with me, but without context. Then I found it in the snapper pie, and letter from Tom.

How many 'moments of real' do you have in your week? Not the pressured meetings, phone calls, emails, SMS messages, Facebook alerts, Instagrams, Snapchats. But real moments of connection – with clients, family, friends, nature, art. Here are moments of real I have relished these past two weeks:

- every morning walking out on to my deck – before the sun fully rises – and feeling the wind. There are messages for us in the wind at dawn

- the conversation I had with Alan over breakfast at our regular café – he's been a client for years, a friend almost as long, and our conversations are as real as they get

- handwriting a 'thank you' note to a stranger (introduced by *Possums* reader and friend Oscar), who made the effort to tell me about something I knew nothing about

- driving colleague Alex from work to my home mid-morning, and then the two of us ran for an hour around the harbour foreshore – talking, marvelling, making plans

- spending an hour with Michelle, a PR industry colleague and competitor for 25 years, catching up, sharing war stories. No posturing, no intrigue, no agenda. Just connection

- my chat with another colleague, where we told each other the truth to the question: 'How are you?' We talked for an hour, and exposed true feelings.

No technology. No pressure. No secret intent. No personal gain. Just moments of real.

It's dawn now. The gum trees are moving. Time to take in the wind's message. Moments of real.

HABITS TO HELP YOU THRIVE

Work on yourself like a project. Work on yourself harder than you do on your job. It's the path to being the very best you can be. It involves developing certain 'habits' that give you the strength, resilience, self-discipline and motivation to keep going – even when you feel dispirited and overwhelmed. It's about managing your own mind, your thoughts and becoming your own very best coach. Here are 12 habits I have developed over my career and life that have helped control my fear, and have inspired me to take the next step forward, even when I have felt like not getting up off the floor.

3.1
LEVERAGE YOUR SPECIAL TALENTS

3.1 A
KNOWING THIS WILL CHANGE YOUR CAREER FOR THE BETTER!

If I'd known this 35 years ago it would have changed my life's path. It's changing it now. I hope this is not too late to positively change yours.

His name is Ken Robinson. Sir Ken. He's an educator. An inspiring speaker. The auditorium at Cannes was packed with 2,000 communications industry executives, eager to hear Sir Ken's 40 minutes on 'How to become more creative'.

In the midst of his speech, Sir Ken shared this insight. It's not complicated. Yet, I'd never realised it before. Now it dominates my thinking about what I do, how I can be happier and how I can contribute more.

Find your element – and work in it every day.

Sir Ken believes each of us have the roles we have because we are good at a number of things important to that specific role.

Some of those things energise us. We're good at and love doing them. They inspire us. When I spend a morning training and coaching young leaders, I finish the session and immediately go for a 10km run. I am on fire. I have energy to burn. I don't want the day to end.

Some of the things we do in our jobs deplete us, even though we're good at them. I lead a series of budget meetings, and do a good job as the hard-nosed guy pushing for more. As soon as the day is over, it's off to the pub for a wine and cigar, shoulders slumped and heart heavy.

Sir Ken's message is to get clear on the things you love to do AND are good at doing. Get better and better at doing these things. Build these increasingly into your role every day. You're then operating in your element. Your energy changes. If you're doing something you love, and you're good at, you get energy from it. If you don't, it takes energy from you.

So, what to do about it?

Think hard about what you do that you're good at, and that you love doing. What are your areas of excellence? What do others say you are really good at doing? What comes naturally to you? Know what makes you come to life. Remember, if you don't love it, you'll never work hard enough to be great. It's about passion and persistence.

Try to reshape your roles so you spend more time working in your element. Sharpen and deepen your skills in these areas. The better you get at these skills, the more you'll be asked to do them. In time, your job fills out just doing stuff you love, and are good at. You're now in your element all the time! Make it your life's work. Create the opportunities you feel you need. Find your best life: your most authentic life that feeds your natural appetite.

Sir Ken reminds us of Thoreau: *'Dwell as near as possible to the channel in which your life flows'*. Make sure you follow this path. You'll have a happier life. And that's a fact!

3.1 B
WHY 'FOLLOW YOUR PASSIONS' IS DANGEROUS ADVICE

I learnt something this week that will stop me from ever encouraging anyone to 'follow their passions'. Oh yes, I've said it many times. Never again. It's just too dangerous advice. Here's why.

I know of several young adults finishing school who are deciding career paths, and university course choices. My advice to them: *'Follow your passions'*. It's the new-age approach, right? Then I actually thought about it. It's deeply flawed counsel. How on earth does a 17-year-old have any clue what their passions are? I'm 54 and am only just getting some clarity on what they might be for me.

Sir Ken Robinson talks about 'working in your element': doing what you love and what you're good at. It's within that concept that the best advice to any younger talent lies. It's not about passion. It's about the other bit.

Follow what you're good at (or could be), and the love will eventually grow.

Cal Newport's idea is to think about what you like doing and could get really good at. Focus on your skill set and competency. Follow your ABILITY, not your passions. You need to be good at something before you can expect a good job. It's sharpening your competency that will find you work that you will eventually love. This is how people end up loving what they do, and working in their element.

Following your passions at an early age is dangerous. It can end up with chronic job shifting, unrelenting angst, and the reality of falling short of dreams. Passions take time to develop and clarify. Just like character.

Rather, develop skills that are rare and valuable to the working world. This is the key currency for creating work you love.

So, whatever age you are, think now about what you like doing and what you are (or could be) good at. Then commit to 'deliberate practice', to keep working on and improving that capability. Make it a mission: a non-negotiable contract with yourself. Keep a growth mindset, always ready to take feedback and improve. Focus your energy on the goal of becoming brilliant at this skill set.

Remember Steve Martin's advice on making it in comedy: *'Be so good they can't ignore you'*.

And if any of this makes sense to you, read more about this brilliant perspective in Cal Newport's *So Good They Can't Ignore You.* I've borrowed heavily from it for this story. It's changed my mind entirely about 'follow your passion'. Sounds great but is almost impossible for someone in the early stages of their career to have any clue how to follow.

Sir Ken again: *'All you want for your kids is for them to find their passion'.* Here's an idea: encourage them to follow their curiosities. Or indeed, to follow abilities and best skills instead. Get brilliant at them. And the joy and passion will come.

3.1 C
ONE CRITICAL DECISION TO TURBOCHARGE YOUR CAREER

Stop spending lots of time trying to improve weaknesses. No kidding. Instead, do this one thing and accelerate your growth and value.

I love feedback, so long as it is positive! I certainly get a lot of it, much of which I don't like.

Consistently through my career I have been told of the areas I need to work on – my 'weaknesses'. There are plenty of them. I've worked hard at fixing them. I have tried. Promise. Really, I have. I've made progress. One inch at a time. I still get feedback on the 'development areas' but not as robustly as before.

Here's my point. And a suggestion for you.

Be less focused on working on 'weaknesses'. Put much more energy into building on your 'strengths'.

I adopted this approach a couple of years ago. It feels great. I figured 100 units of effort on working on a weakness might take me from being poor at something to being just below average. But 100 units of effort working on building a clear strength would take me from being really good at something, to becoming 'fricking awesome' at it.

Employers and clients want 'fricking awesome'. They will pay extra for it. So long as your 'weaknesses' are not socially unacceptable or dramatically undermine the good stuff, they'll forgive you for them.

Not all will agree. Some will say: *'NO! STOP! Practising our strengths and ignoring our weaknesses is a failing. Your strengths will only take you as far as your weaknesses will allow'.*

I don't agree. Leonard Cohen puts it well: *'Don't paint stripes on your back if you're not a zebra. Focus on building upon your unique abilities'.*

Getting hung up on weaknesses is a black hole to nowhere. Sure, know your weaknesses, accept them, and work consistently and with effort to make progress to soften their dark shadow.

But put the passion, big energy, enthusiasm and extra hard yards into making your strengths unbelievably great. Play to your strengths. Strengthen your strengths. Know what your clients or company most value you for, and then get better and better at it.

What is the one skill you have that, if you worked on it, could become 'fricking awesome'? Come on now – don't be shy. Shout it out. Then, get to work. Become absolutely brilliant at it: famous for it. No excuses. Get cracking!

3.1 D
HOW TO GET WHAT YOU WANT – EVERY TIME!

There's something I do at the start of meetings that often shocks those there. Some love it. Others hate it. It's a recipe for getting what you want.

My working day is filled with meetings. Some I set up. Usually, given my current role, it's others who have asked to see me: colleagues, potential partners, industry associates, general contacts. I have to move through them efficiently. I must make sure we get to the point quickly if I am to add value.

I often start meetings others have asked for with this question: *'If you had a magic wand, what would happen at the end of the meeting: what is it you want me to think or do?'* It's a concept I encourage you to embrace. Do it for yourselves. This is what I mean.

Boldly ask for what you want.

I want my meeting guests to boldly tell me what they want, right up front.

Cut out the long-winded preambles, vague indications, hints, evasive approaches.

Don't be rude, pushy or nagging. Be grounded in reality on what's possible and fair. But, all provisos and small print aside, do have courage. Ask clearly, politely, respectfully, yet firmly for what you want. One of two things will happen when you do this.

1. You get what you want – or close to it

Your bosses or colleagues are not mind readers. They are not thinking about you as much as you are thinking about you. Give them the clear compass point. Make sure it's a reasonable ask, achievable and fair. Maybe it's on the edge a little; perhaps you're pushing it a step beyond the reasonable, but ask anyway. There is a good chance you will get it, or most of it, given you're in good shape as a brand and 'value proposition' to whomever you're asking.

2. You won't get it

That's good too. You get clarity. Ask for something you feel is fair and you really want, and you get a 'no', then you know where you stand. You either suck it up, or you exit stage left. One door closes, many others open.

Stop wasting time and angst. Have courage. Ask boldly for what you want. Do it elegantly. And be prepared to get a 'no'. That is progress too.

There is of course a risk. I have seen people misjudge their 'brand' health and standing with their employer to such an extent that when they boldly ask for something, they get a very negative reaction. It can bring to a head something their employer was thinking of doing anyway. That's brutal, but it happens.

One idea to help build the courage is have a clear plan on what you will say and do if you do get a 'no'. In this way, there's no fear, no panic. You have a plan. You're ready. Breathe deeply. Go forth.

If you trust your judgment, are level-headed, grounded and have the courage of your convictions, then ASK. Good things come from it. That's from my heart. (It even worked out okay in the end for Oliver Twist, right?)

3.1 E
HAVE THE COURAGE TO ANSWER THIS ONE QUESTION

This is a short, sharp story. It's designed to get you thinking.
Beware – it might scare you. Do you have the courage to tell the truth?
I wonder.

All my life I have been handcuffed by insecurity and self-doubt.

I have tried to compensate by being 'extroverted'. I appear confident
and strong. It's a façade. Just under the surface is a person frightened
of failure, the unknown, risk, ridicule. Fear and shame have
underpinned most of what I have and haven't done in my life.

I am a little better at it now. I still got a shock, though, when
confronted with this very basic question.

What would you do now if you knew you could not fail?

I heard that challenge in a bad movie, *New Year's Eve* I think it was. It
resonated. I wrote it down. Thought about it. What would I do now in
my life if I knew I could not fail? Incredibly hard to answer, truthfully.
I'll tell you what I came up with, but first a question for you.

Your challenge: *What would you do right now in your life if you knew you
could not fail?*

It was this question that creative leader Bruce Matchett countered
with an even more powerful thought. It forces us to get very clear on
what we really, really want to do every day. It is similar to my previous
ask, but sharper, better. Here it is. Give it a go.

*If every job in the world paid $50,000, what job would you do if you could
do any job?*

Think about it. Honestly.

What would I do? If I had my time again, or knew for sure if I quit now
I could reinvent myself and retain my standard of living, I'd become a

garden designer. I'd be good at it, and love doing it. Working on and in gardens is my happiest time. I'd love to do that all the time.

So what to do next? Well, I suppose I can start thinking about how to make that dream come true. Maybe I can start studying part time, or get a part-time job working with a garden designer. Perhaps I could get a garden designer as a client? That would be fun! Make a start. Take a step. Plenty of time to change course. But will I do it? Do I have the guts to give it a go? Probably not, sadly.

I am having too much fun now, and the risk is just too great. BUT, then again, if I knew I could not fail ... What about you?

3.2

STAY CONNECTED, PASSIONATELY

3.2 A
USHER, TATTOOS, TAXIS –
THREE TIPS TO KEEP OTHERS WANTING MORE

Being in the mosh pit at rock concerts makes you a better, more relevant, 'in demand' and vibrant professional. Sounds weird? Maybe, but it's true.

Pink's was bouncy, young, optimistic, inspiring. Kings of Leon grungy, alcohol-fuelled and smelling of vomit. I saw stuff at Usher I am still trying to process! Leonard Cohen? The crowd was so old we were all seated! But there was a vibe of thoughtfulness and gratitude there I had never felt before. Point is, I learnt an enormous amount at each event.

We have to work daily to 'feed our minds' and keep connected to the real world: the audiences and subcultures our clients or organisations are selling products to. Before I share three tips to do just that, ask yourself this.

Do you live in a 'nice' suburb, travel to work every day using the same mode of transport and same route, listen to the same couple of radio stations, read the same weekly magazines, watch the same TV shows, visit a small group of websites regularly, eat at a favourite handful of restaurants, order the same dishes often, mix with the same group most of the time? Sound familiar?

Clients and colleagues expect us to 'know stuff': about what's happening today, and what's coming around the corner. To be 'in the groove', connected to trends, events, the street. They want to know our ideas are built on genuine insights, that we are engaged and connected: that we are alive!

Leading predictable lives, living in our comfort zones and seeking the familiar is an easy trap to fall into. Big mistake if you want to grow clients, and keep your careers vibrant. Here are the three ways I stay connected.

1. *Read stuff I am not interested in:* A Tom Peters idea. Read magazines on topics you have NO interest in. The last time I caught a plane I bought *Tattoos R Us, Weddings Weekly* and *Kite Flyers Monthly* (not real names, but you get the idea). All topics I am currently not interested in. I read them with a passion, underlining, tearing stuff out, noting people to follow on Twitter, and so on. Do this and within a month you will have used knowledge learnt from those magazines in value-adding ways with clients.

2. *Get into the 'mosh pit', often:* Whether a rock concert or movie festival, a suburb you have never been to, a parade or local market. Turn up! Look at who is there: what people are wearing, their mobile devices, how they use them, their make-up, hairstyles, jewellery, what they are drinking, talking about, how they interact. Think of your clients. Where is the lesson? Where's the magic? Jonathan Pease (@jonathanpease) does this when he travels: soaks up sights, sounds and culture, and uses the valuable lessons in service of his clients.

3. *Talk to taxi drivers:* I learnt this from Rose Herceg. Talk to cabbies. Ask them what's happening, how is business, what their passengers are talking about, what they think about politician X, what they are listening to? What's their story, what is their life like,

what do they like and not like about the city/country? Dig deep. Be empathetic. Listen intently. Be genuinely interested. Drink it in.

Order dishes at restaurants you would normally never order. Ask colleagues what they are reading and why. Go into stores you have no reason to. Walk down a new street. Go watch a game of a sport you don't know well. You get the picture. Oh, and READ NEWSPAPERS – online or off. Every day.

TURN UP to staying connected and current. Make it a priority every day. It makes you a more valuable contributor, for longer.

3.2 B
TAKE THIS ONE LIFE-CHANGING ACTION EVERY DAY

I am weak. I promised myself three years ago I would do this, every day. It's so valuable for an engaged and exciting life. I have failed. I have not had the guts to do it.

Peter Cullinane, founder of New Zealand's Assignment, suggested *Fun While it Lasted* by Barnaby Conrad: a true story of how an American in the 1940s became a matador in Spain. One of Barnaby's hobbies was collecting notable deathbed utterings. He ends his book quoting a woman whose last words were: *'Well, it's all been very interesting'.*

On reading this, I realised a part of my life was an opportunity missed. I am a creature of habit. My life just isn't always 'interesting'. What I promised myself three years ago was I would do this:

Do something every day that scares you.

I liked Eleanor Roosevelt's suggestion.

'Yes I will. I'll do it!' I thought about what I had done in recent years that had 'scared me'. I am ashamed to say the list was short. Three years later, and it is still short.

I have to attack this head on.

This is not about swimming with sharks or bungee jumping. It's about small steps of personal risk to add flavour and diversity, and to push through fears and inhibitions. Here's my list for the next month. What's yours?

- Commit to five meditation sessions in one week (anxiety building already)

- Turn off my technology for two hours a day, every day

- Tell three people daily I appreciate and am grateful for what they do for me

- Go sit in a church, mosque or synagogue for an hour and just be present

- Go see a nutritionist.

Not the most exciting list in the world, but every item scares me. Really. Doing this would be BIG progress.

A final thought. Françoise Gilot was Picasso's mistress from 1942 to 1953. *'I knew of Picasso's reputation with women and knew that moving in with him would be a catastrophe – but I decided it was a catastrophe I didn't want to miss.'* Sometimes we need to make sure we don't miss the catastrophe. Take risk. Push yourself beyond your comfort levels.

At the Cannes Creativity Festival in June 2011, Google chairman Eric Schmidt talked about: *'Try to say "yes"'*. Black Eyed Peas front man will.i.am said: *'Take personal risk. Take a step forward. Be bold'*.

If we heed their advice, even with small first steps, then maybe we'll have last words of: *'Well, it's all been very interesting'*.

Postscript

I'm proud of myself. I just quit my big-power, big-rewards job. Why? Because I was in a comfort zone. I needed to take a 'big step' forward. To take personal risk. Have to say, the heart is beating faster and butterflies abound. It feels great! Well done, Chris! I am proud of you.

3.2 C
THE MOST EXCITING HABIT IN LIFE – ENJOY IT OFTEN

I was in the taco queue at the Bruce Springsteen concert when the guy behind me said something totally inspiring. It reminded me of what makes for an exciting and connected life, and an awesome career.

Former colleague Rose was frustrated. *'I was sitting next to a dull man at lunch. There is just no excuse for dullness. DO SOMETHING! Stand for something! Get connected to something. Believe in something! Fail massively at something! Have something to say!!! Just whatever you do, don't be dull!'* It struck a chord. Then while in the taco queue, an American voice behind me said to his companion: *'Oh yes, I was here last night. I travelled here from Hawaii for these concerts. I am a huge Bruce fan. Tonight is the 152nd time I have seen him live'.*

That Springsteen devotee had something in his life we all need. It's what Rose was looking for. Without it, we are dull: in life, at work, in everything. Here it is.

Make sure you have 'great enthusiasms' in your life – always.

Toad of Toad Hall had constant 'great enthusiasms'. He'd get hugely passionate, obsessed, loving every second of it, shooting up like a rocket, and crashing to earth a burnt stick. That's okay too. You don't have to do '152 live gigs' with every passion. It's fine to park them, and move on.

There's an 11-year-old I know. He's like Toad. Huge waves of enthusiasm: *Star Wars*, LEGO, football, cricket, *Top Gear*. He gets totally enthusiastic, buys the gear, downloads the apps, sticks up posters, knows all the names, the songs. He moves from one to the other seamlessly. Packs away one lot of gear, dusts off another, and away he goes. 100% raw, unadulterated passion, every time.

Then there's Peter. He is passionate around every single event, every day. When he cooks pasta, he does it with Italian opera pumping, olives to nibble, ice cold Peronis at hand, and a bold Chianti breathing for the main course. All followed by a rip-roaring Italian classic movie to stir the juices. You ARE Italian for those three hours.

Apart from family, for me it's about making a difference and leaving a legacy of inspiration with people I care about, learning and growing, grand old colonial-style hotels, gardens, Leonard Cohen. The list goes on. Lots of enthusiasms, little depth in any. I like it that way.

What about you? Do you have full-on, hard-core, heart-thumping, yelp out loud, *'goddam I just LOVE this'* passions: enthusiasms that excite and fulfil, that grow, evolve, that keep you engaged and connected? List them out now. Do you spend enough time enjoying and exploring them? Or are you the dull person Rose sat next to at lunch last week? Come on now – the truth.

Postscript

Alex and Anouk both shared this Theodore Roosevelt quote with me. It's worth a read. I know who I want to be.

'It is not the critic who counts; not the man who points out how the strong man stumbles, or where the doer of deeds could have done them better. The credit belongs to the man who is actually in the arena, whose face is marred by dust and sweat and blood, who strives valiantly; who errs and comes short again and again; because there is not effort without error and shortcomings; but who does actually strive to do the deed; who knows the great enthusiasm, the great devotion, who spends himself in a worthy cause, who at the best knows in the end the triumph of high achievement and who at the worst, if he fails, at least he fails while daring greatly. So that his place shall never be with those cold and timid souls who know neither victory nor defeat.'

3.2 D
WHY I HAVE THE BEST JOB IN THE WORLD –
AND YOU CAN TOO!

This story might shape your career, or change your path forever. It's about staying constantly connected to how you feel about your job, and how to best manage career choices.

It will help tell you whether you have the best job in the world. Or if it's time to move on.

My girlfriend and I were looking to buy a terrace home in Sydney's inner west. We viewed an evening inspection. Fairy lights were strung through the trees, twinkling away. Exquisite. Captivating! We wanted it, badly!

Her Hungarian stepfather arrived. He took me aside. *'Beware the pretty lights,'* he warned. The building inspection proved him right. Under the surface, the place was a wreck. Since then, whenever an opportunity has winked and seemed oh so attractive, I have remembered his words:

Beware the pretty lights.

We have one shot at our careers. The roles to which we give our talents and energies must give us what we need to thrive, be fulfilled, happy and to achieve our potential. Often we get jaded in our jobs, and are tempted by a new role offering plenty of 'pretty lights'. Pause a moment. Stay connected to your real feelings. Can you improve conditions of your current role to make it better for you at this stage of your career?

Here are my 'big five' criteria which make up the ideal job. Look at each. Think about your job right now. How do you feel about each criterion? Score each out of 10. Add it up at the end for a total score out of 50.

- *Make a difference:* Am I making a valuable, real difference? Am I contributing, bringing something fresh, helping to make the business better? Think about your current role: are you doing this? Score it out of 10 – 1/10 being *'I never make a difference'* and 10/10 being *'I make a massive difference every day'*.

- *Learn and grow:* Am I learning and growing in my role? Doug Smollan, chairman of field marketing leader Smollan Group, answered *'Doug, what's driven your success?'* with *'I stayed green. Don't get ripe. You rot and fall off the tree. Ensure you are challenged and learning, and whatever you do brings you new personal growth'.* Are you learning and growing in your role? Score it out of 10.

- *Have fun:* Do I love what I do? Is it fun? Or do I drag myself out of bed to go to 'work'? I have 'worked' very few days in my career. Instead, it's been an adventure of challenge, success, failure and camaraderie. I've been blessed with working with wonderful people, 'pirates' who love to laugh. What fun we've had! 1/10 you hate it, 10/10 you absolutely love it.

- *Right for my life:* Does the role give me what I need for the other very important things in my life? Family, health, interests, passions? Are you able to have appropriate balance, whatever 'balance' means to you? Does your role give you what you need to lead a 'whole' life? Score out of 10?

- *Rewards are fair:* Are the rewards fair and reasonable given what I contribute, and compared to industry standards? Think hard about what we earn and how that 'fits' with the role and industry. We can always earn 15–20% more elsewhere. That's not the point. Put that out of your mind. The issue is fairness and reasonableness in your current role. Score out of 10?

What did you score overall? Did you get close to 35/50? I reckon that's a 'pass' mark. If not, don't worry. It does not mean you're in the wrong role. With a little bit of thought and dialogue, you can improve scores of individual pillars quickly. Focus on making a good role GREAT. Make the grass greener on **this** side of the fence.

Remember – all five criteria don't need to be 'perfect' all the time. There will always be ups and downs – periods when it's not fun, the balance is bad, you're grinding not learning, and you're underpaid.

If overall you keep the average at over 35 out of 50, well – frankly – I reckon that's a pretty special role. Keep it if you've got it. Or take it if what you're being offered seems to be able to give it to you. But, please beware the pretty lights!

Postscript

A colleague rejects the 'work-life' balance concept. *'It's all my life, and I want it all to be great,'* she says. Whereas Tom Moult, the then chairman of Ogilvy Australia, took on this massive role in early 2011 because in his previous role, where he was working part time, *'I had a problem with my work-life balance: I was getting too much life!'*

Here's an interesting perspective on 'balance'. *'If you know what you most value, what is most important to you in your life, and you are spending the right amount of time on each, then you have the balance.'*

3.3
BE OPTIMISTIC

3.3 A
HOW TO KEEP STRONG WHEN THE PRESSURE IS ON

I gave a presentation to a room of colleagues. I got to a slide I'd presented a thousand times, and yet its message struck me hard, as if I was hearing it for the first time. It was a message of hope, and of resilience.

Our lives and roles can't always be a bowl of cherries. Sometimes pressure builds, tensions rise, relationships get tested. Constant pressure depletes energy. It pulls you down, clouds judgment. You can feel trapped in the relentlessness of it all. The fun goes. Life becomes a grind. Know what I mean?

Pressure makes me intensely irritable. I comfort eat. I lose excitement and hope about the future. Then slide 17 reminded me of this advice. I have used it to lift my spirits. Perhaps it can help you do the same when you are feeling the pinch.

The happiest people in the world have trained themselves to become 'learned optimists'.

Train yourself to react positively to the things that happen to you: to each setback, body blow, or issue of the day. It can become an energising, empowering habit. *'When you change the way you look at things, the things you look at change.'*

Armed with this reminder to choose to react with optimism to setbacks, I then worked out what else I could do to pivot my dark mood. I needed to move from a sense of diminished hope, of entrapment, to one of increasing optimism, empowerment, freedom, energised intent.

So, I resolved to try to respond with cheerfulness to every problem that came my way.

Leonard Cohen said: *'I have tried all the religions of the world, but cheerfulness keeps breaking through.'*

Sometimes we just take things too fricking seriously. Instead of reacting to issues with furrowed brow, I have resolved to react with a smile and a sense of adventure. It's not life and death. As Steve Jobs said: *'Remembering you're going to die is the best way I have found to avoid the trap of thinking you have something to lose.'*

John Gardner, the founder of investor relations firm MAGNUS (now rebadged Citadel – MAGNUS), is the most optimistic guy I know. When he worked with me at Savage & Partners, John's optimism saved me from giving up. A big banking client called to fire us. I put the phone down, devastated. *'But that's great news,'* said John, enthusiastically. *'Yes, we will miss the revenue short term, but they were a difficult client, marginally profitable, did not appreciate us, and we all hated working on it. Now we are free to work for their competitor!'* And that's exactly what we did, in time, with enthusiasm, a spring in our step, and hope in our hearts.

Get things into perspective. Problems and issues are just turbulence along your fast-moving journey. Tackle them with humour, enthusiasm, and a sense of playfulness. Remember: it just does not matter that much. Become a learned optimist. *'When you change the way you look at things, the things you look at change.'*

3.3 B
THREE INGREDIENTS TO HAPPINESS –
AT WORK AND IN LIFE

'85% of the secret to success is just turning up.' I 'turned up' to a talk by someone billed as *'the worldwide expert on happiness'*. An hour later I was a changed man. And have had a much happier life ever since. Here are the three key tips I learnt that day.

Dr Martin Seligman is the director of the Positive Psychology Center at the University of Pennsylvania. He's spent much of his career helping people suffering from depression. Through this work he gained deep insight into 'happiness' and resilience, which has shaped theories that I wanted to hear about.

So one cold winter night I went to his lecture in downtown Sydney. It was enlightening.

This is how I recall what he told us, and how I have used it to help shape my life. I share these three tips at every training session I lead. I tell my friends. I tell my children.

The 'happiest' people Seligman observes have three common characteristics:

- *They do every day what they love and what they are good at.*
  A very similar message to Sir Ken Robinson's *'Work in your element'*. Be clear about what you really love doing most and are good at, and build that into your working life as much as you can. I have not worked many days in my life. I am lucky. I love work, challenges, working with young people, and the creative industries. I'm in my element when I coach and inspire. I get to do that every day.

- *They do something for others without expecting anything back in return.*
  I do this by helping as many young people as possible make a start in this industry. I give them time, and link them with my contacts, hoping to kick-start momentum to finding a role. Increasingly I am doing this with the older tribe, trying to reinvent themselves and find relevant roles and longevity in the latter phases of careers.

- *They are optimists, and have learnt to stay that way.*
  Seligman calls it learned optimism. It's this concept I tell all and
  sundry. Train yourself to be optimistic in how you view the world,
  and how you react to circumstance. Become a skilled 'disputer of
  negative thoughts.' (You know, when that voice tells you: *'You can't
  do it – it will be a disaster'*. Counter it with: *'Hang on a minute – yes
  I CAN do it. It will be great, and I am absolutely going to give it a go')*.
  Take full responsibility for what happens to you. Refuse to blame
  other people. Learn lessons from setbacks. Keep looking forward for
  actions you can take to improve matters. Have hope.

Be optimistic. Train yourself to view the world that way. Focus on
what you can do next. It makes for a much happier life. That's how
becoming a learned optimist has impacted mine.

3.3 C
THIS WILL HELP YOU TRIUMPH IN TOUGH TIMES

Wow! The year has started with breath-taking change, challenge and opportunity. It's intense. To cope with turbulent, uncharted waters, we need one thing constantly by our side. Without it, we won't make it.

Former Australian prime minister Paul Keating is passionate about the power of confidence.

'Confidence,' he says, *'is not something you can get by every now and then swallowing a can of "confidence" spinach. It has to be continually with you.'* He believes confidence comes from experience. Confidence also comes from something every one of us has within our grasp. You have it. I have it. I do it. Always. Do you? I hope so. Here it is.

Confidence is preparation.

That's it. If you prepare thoroughly, you will gain huge confidence. There will be butterflies. Palms will moisten. But you will have eagerness in your stride to get into the challenge. Confidence gives you strength and optimism. In fact, success happens when preparation meets opportunity.

Constantly over the past 30 years I have 'won' the moment, nailed the meeting, landed the sale, smoothed through the difficult discussion, blitzed the incredibly action-packed day of major deliverables, not because I was smarter, more talented, gifted, blessed or lucky but because I was really well prepared. When I stuffed up, it was always because I was not prepared.

Here are three tips to build, maintain and protect confidence:

1. Preparation delivers confidence

It's the golden rule. As you face pressure and challenges, think carefully about how you can best PREPARE. What research can you do, how can you uncover a genuine insight, who can help you, how can you 'role play' in your mind everything that could transpire and how you will handle each moment? Sweat the detail in preparation.

2. Take a step back if you feel you are losing the edge

Cricket great Sir Geoff Boycott says that to build confidence, sometimes you have to go back to basics, and start preparing from the start again. *'A Test cricketer who has lost confidence needs to go back to county cricket and work on the basics, prepare afresh, and rebuild.'* If, for example, you feel your presenting style is off its game, give a few talks to low-risk internal meetings. Rebuild confidence 'back in county cricket' so you are on your game for that major new business pitch when the stakes are high. Nothing builds confidence faster than getting more competent.

3. Controlling the demons in your mind

'Believe you can and you are halfway there.' So said Theodore Roosevelt. Sometimes, no matter how much I prepare, there's a voice that keeps whispering to me: *'You're kidding Chris: you will fail here, no question'.*

To build confidence, we have to become 'brilliant disputers of negative thoughts'. The *'No I can't ...'* needs to be immediately countered with *'That's rubbish – of course I can. It is in my grasp'.*

It's Sunday night. I have a week of important presentations around Australia. I need to plan every meeting, role-play in my mind, start rehearsing, think how I will maximise the times I have in cabs and at airports, prepare for what can go wrong. You see, preparation gives me confidence. Confidence keeps me excited and believing 'anything is possible'. Always has. Always will.

3.3 D
I AM ASHAMED OF MY GREATEST FAILING –
BUT I AM BEATING IT

What do WD-40 (a type of grease lubricant), a successful entrepreneur and my greatest failing in life have in common? Calm down! This is NOT an R-rated story. It's about fear.

I had breakfast with an inspiring, successful entrepreneur, Creel Price. He sold one of his businesses a few years ago for $100 million (he paid for breakfast).

'Creel developed his serial entrepreneurial nature from the age of 11 when he started a strawberry business that within two years was employing both his parents. Creel recently established the Club Kidpreneur Foundation, a social enterprise committed to assisting youths start and grow their own micro-enterprises in order that one day they may choose entrepreneurship as a career.'

'What's the point of Kidpreneur?' I asked. His answer summed up one of my greatest failings, and fears.

Learn early that it is okay to fail; and use setbacks to build resilience.

Not exactly his words, but the essence. *Learn early about failing.* Build an ability to cope with failure and setbacks. Take their valuable lessons, and move forward with determination and optimism.

Creel made me think about how much opportunity and experience I have missed because I am often paralysed by a fear of failure. How could I have approached coping with failure better?

Later, I researched what others have to say about fear of failure. The consensus? Failure is a key ingredient of success: *'Failure is the path to success.' 'Fail. Fail again. Fail better.' 'We either learn to fail, or we fail to learn.' 'The way to succeed is to double your error rate.' 'The question is not whether we fail or not; the question is how much we fail and what we do with failure.' 'A high failure rate is a hallmark of creative genius.'* And, from the JWT induction book, quoting Edward Phelps: *'The man who makes no mistakes, does not usually make anything'.*

I realised 'failure' was the wrong word to describe what happens when things don't work out. *'Making mistakes is how we learn, and fear of them can be a huge barrier to success.'* Winston Churchill learnt his lesson early. It made him. When we 'fail' it's simply a speed bump on our journey, like turbulence for a powerful jet aircraft shooting through the skies.

Treat every setback and challenge as an opportunity to learn. If something fails, learn from it, move on, and try hard not to repeat the mistake. And move on with gratefulness and optimism pumping through your veins.

Easier said than done. Granted. But it can be done.

What is your biggest fear holding you back right now, and how are you going to manage to beat it?

Postscript

I was telling my friend Russell about this story, fearing it would not be compelling. *'Fear not,'* he soothed. *'Tell the story of WD-40, the lubricant. The name stands for "water displacement – 40th attempt".'* Its inventor arrived at a successful formula on his 40th attempt. He was so proud of his resilience in accepting setbacks, learning from them and moving forward, that he named the product after it!

3.4
YOU ARE YOUR SCHEDULE

3.4 A
WHY EATING FROGS NEEDS TO BE A DAILY HABIT

I read eating a live frog every morning would help me achieve more. I tried it. It's not pleasant, but it sure as heck works.

If anyone ever asked my view on the key to success in business, my answer I fear would disappoint. Yet this one habit has driven whatever success I have had in my little world.

It's helped me stay one step ahead and get the opportunities that have come my way. It might leave you underwhelmed. So be it. Try not to shout out 'huh?' when I say this obsessive, magical habit is:

To-do lists.

That's the secret. To-do lists: well planned; carefully prioritised; obsessively and ruthlessly followed every day.

Get more of the important things done every day. Don't work harder or longer. Just get your priorities right. And be relentless in sticking to them. Become the most productive person you know. Here's how:

- *Plan your day in advance:* Every evening I plan my next day. When are my meetings? Am I ready for them? What are my goals? I make a long list of all the things I need to get done. Plan to use every minute. Use all the nooks and crannies of time. (I'm writing this while waiting to leave a London hotel to visit Madame Tussauds. Just 15 minutes, but a nook and cranny of time to make progress!)

- *Identify your Big Rock:* Then I identify the most critical task I MUST DO that will make the most powerful impact on my job and on the way I feel. I call it my Big Rock. Brian Tracy calls it his 'Frog' in his outstanding book, *Eat That Frog*. I've bought hundreds of copies of this book over the years and given them to colleagues. Brian's theory goes something like this:

  'Eating a live frog every morning is likely to be the worst thing that will happen to you that day. Every night, work out what is the one thing – no matter what else happens – that you simply MUST get done or make progress on the next day ... the one thing that will make the most difference to your job and peace of mind ... that's your FROG. Get started on it first thing when you get to work.'

  I work out exactly what that Frog, or Big Rock, is. I make it the very first action of my business day. And if you have two Big Rock or Frogs for the next day? Well, Tracy says, *'eat the ugliest one first!'*

- *Prioritise:* I then identify my four As, and prioritise them. A1, A2, A3, A4. Then my four Bs: B1, B2, B3, B4. I also note all the other stuff it would be nice to get done.

- *Write the list:* Then I write the list (on a piece of paper – not electronically). I first list the Big Rock (which I highlight in pink highlighter). Then the four As and the four Bs. Then the rest.

- *Follow the list 'like a terrier on steroids':* The most critical step then is to stick to your priorities relentlessly. I start first always on the Big Rock, making as much progress as I can – ideally finishing it. Move on to the A1. The phone rings. It happens to be – say – a B3 priority on the list. Get it done and tick it off. Then finish the A1.

Move on to the A2. Finish that. A client calls. Urgent issue – so then create a new A1. Get it done. Go back to the list. Aha – I'm at A3 – so I get it moving. Stick to your list. Yes – be flexible to deal with the 'issues of the day'. But keep coming back to your list. And stick to the priorities! This is the key. Relentlessly. Obsessively. Passionately. Make it a personal challenge every day to cross off your list as much as you can, in the right order. And it's okay to re-do the list at lunchtime – refresh the priorities based on what's happened so far that day.

The day ends. Review your list. 90% of what you needed to do – the most important stuff – is done. Start again. Think about tomorrow. Plan the day. Make a long list. Identify the Big Rock. I know it's simple. But it works.

Postscript

To-do lists and prioritising, and then sticking to your priorities, is without doubt the most valuable business tip I know. And frankly a 'life' tip. It's a habit best started early in life. When I was 14, my mother found a list I had written – the ultimate list. It was titled: *List of Lists I Need To Make*. Enough said. Nothing gave me more pleasure than seeing over the weekend a *Things To Do Today* prioritised list on the desk of a 16-year-old mate. That's despite the fact her Big Rock was *'ask Dad to give me $50'*. Damn!

3.4 B
I RUINED MY MOST VALUABLE ASSET –
HAVE YOU RUINED YOURS?

I have always taken on too much. The control freak in me? Or an incredible insecurity to prove myself? I dread not keeping promises or repaying even a $10 debt, and am obsessed with lists and productivity. Frankly – I've screwed up massively. Don't make this same mistake. Please.

Too much to do. Never enough time. Know that feeling? It does not matter how hard and efficiently I work, I have a never decreasing set of lists needing action – on aspects of my job, my family, home, health, finances, networks. The lists go on. I work relentlessly. My days are filled with meetings – that's part of my role; there is no shortage of senior colleagues who ask for time, clients who demand it or industry contacts to keep in touch with.

It often seems impossible to 'fit it all in'. This sage advice from a business tycoon I heard at a conference I was speaking at in Africa gives us the answer. It has revolutionised my thinking. This is what he said:

Only do what only you can do.

Simple. Insightful. Profound. Only do what ONLY YOU can do. So:

First, every week, sit quietly for 10 minutes. Get clarity on your Big Rocks for the week or month ahead. What are the four to six major projects you need to be engaged in and driving?

Second, when I review my to-do lists for the next day or week, or someone wants a meeting, I now pause and double check: *'Do I really need to do that? Can a colleague just as effectively (or indeed, often, much better) handle that?'* Most of the time the answer is: *'No need for you, big fella'.*

Third, double check again: if you have decided *'no, not needed'*, just cross reference it to your Big Rocks and ensure your decision does not undermine critical priorities.

'Only do what only you can do.' It's made a real and powerful difference. Give it a try!

Postscript

Former Ogilvy Australia chairman, Tom Moult, shared his approach: *'Don't let the urgent get in the way of the important'.* That's another great concept. As former US president Dwight Eisenhower said: *'What is important is seldom urgent and what is urgent is seldom important.'*

Focus on your important and urgent tasks. Then the important and not urgent (often this is where the longer-term value is created for your business). Then, and only then, turn to the most distracting of all, the urgent but NOT important tasks. And then of course those not urgent and not important tasks that suck up so much time. STOP DOING THEM ALTOGETHER!!!!

Right, enough already: that's another not urgent and not overly important job done.

3.4 C
THE SIMPLE TRUTH ABOUT HOW TO BE MORE EFFECTIVE

Here's a challenge. It will take one minute, and WILL make a huge difference to your ability to achieve goals and success in what you do. Up for it?

I was in Ho Chi Minh City. My colleague presented an impressive plan to improve performance across the business. It was well thought out. Comprehensive. All the right actions were there. About 12 things that needed to be done. The team was aligned.

At this point I would normally have said: *'Ebne – excellent, but not enough'*. Instead, I thought to myself *'EBTA – excellent, but too ambitious'*. So I challenged the team to do something extremely hard to do: to do LESS. Here's why.

Simplicity is the highest form of achievement.

The Ho Chi Minh City plan was too extensive: and not ruthlessly prioritised. What I asked my colleagues to do was this: *'Select just three things. The most critical actions that will make the most impact. Put every ounce of effort behind those. Implement them brilliantly. Do that before doing anything else on the list'.*

We HAVE to simplify everything we do. You can do anything, but not everything. Stop trying to do things better. Instead, do fewer things better.

'Simplicity is the ultimate sophistication,' said Da Vinci. And, dammit, it is! Simplicity demonstrates remarkable elegance. Learn to let go. The best writers will tell you they edit, edit again, and keep on editing. If a word can be left out, then delete it. If in doubt, take it out.

Arianna Huffington is a big fan of simplicity. She relieves pressure by selecting projects to drop: things she planned to do that are creating unnecessary pressure. She drops them altogether.

Now, I am certainly no poster child for simplicity.

But it's okay. I've made a start. You can too. Do less, and get more from it. Clarity comes from simplicity. Our lives are frittered away with detail and complexity. Complexity creates pressure. STOP. Simplify. Simplify. Simplify.

3.4 D
HOW TO HAVE MORE TIME IN YOUR LIFE – AND IT WORKS!

A book winks at me daily from my bookcase. *In Praise of Slowness: Challenging the Cult of Speed.* Problem is, I have been too flat out to read it. I now have the answer to finding that time. It works. Do you have it?

I also have *The Power of Less: The Fine Art of Limiting Yourself to the Essential ... in Business and in Life.* I haven't read that either. No time. Too much else to do. Let's hope it's not essential reading!

I pride myself on my relentlessness. Today is a case in point: a huge 'urgent and important' to-do list, plus a *Possums* post to write. How am I going to get it all done?

Then I remembered colleague Alan's advice. While he too is driven by to-do lists, he's even more obsessed with this tip to being effective and efficient.

He clarifies, daily, his 'to-don't' list.

What are the things we WON'T do in the next day, week, or at all. Yes, a clear, prioritised to-do list is vital for productivity and effectiveness. Follow that priority list, relentlessly.

Then sprinkle Alan's idea across everything you do. Clarify what you WON'T do every day. Avoid things that suck up time and are not 'mission critical'.

CMO Andy suggested this refinement. When preparing a to-do list, allocate how much time you will spend against each action. It's a sharp idea. Keeps you focused. You get more done.

Here's another idea. Don't prioritise what's on your schedule. Rather, schedule your priorities. Big difference. Being able to solve problems is nowhere near as important as picking the right problems to solve. Focus on big problems – where the big impact is. Change the allocation of your time.

With this in mind, I have been reflecting on what I do and how I do it. How can I best add value? This was my insight: *I will DO less, and lead more.*

I will make sure I am working on fewer, bigger actions to deliver the most impact to clients, businesses, colleagues, momentum, family, for me. I will only do what only I can do in that process.

Won't be easy. Or perfect. There's no growth in perfection anyway. If I can get this 50% right, then I have to believe I will get time back. I might even be able to read a book that has been winking at me!

3.4 E
DELIVER MAXIMUM VALUE TO YOUR ROLE – EVERY DAY!

Like to earn more money? Would a promotion be nice too? For many, just knowing they are making a BIG contribution and are valued are the most powerful drivers. How do you get all three? Appreciation, more money, bigger roles? Here's a simple idea that works.

The answer to this question will tell you if you have a worthy role: *'Do I make a valuable and powerful difference?'* What a bummer if we turned up every day and our contribution to our businesses was marginal. Making sure we add value, consistently, needs constant reassessment. It needs to become a habit.

It is easy to get stuck in marginal–value activity. I do it, often. Here is how to stop this happening.

Ask yourself this question daily, and then deliver hard on the answer. Do this and you will continue to make a powerful difference.

What is the one thing I can get done today that will bring the most value to this business?

Get clear on the answer. Then get cracking on the delivery. Do it every day.

It is not easy. It needs constant review. Here is my just invented *Four Point Plan* to consistently deliver 'insane' value. Not sure it works, but I am giving it a go:

1. Make an appointment with yourself every week. Call it your 'Hour of ROI Power'. The return on investment is for your company: it's about how to give maximum value in the week ahead.

2. In the 'Hour of ROI Power', ask yourself these questions:

   a. Why am I on the payroll?

   b. What is the highest–value use of my time?

c. How can I increase the value of my service to my company today, and for the coming week?

d. What can I, and only I, do that, if done well, can make a real difference?

3. Check in with your boss or colleagues on what you have concluded. Do they agree?

4. Then get focused on delivering that plan, every day.

Do the really important things well. Focus relentlessly on what adds REAL value. It is easy to get 'lost' in the hurly-burly of day-to-day combat. You need to routinely pause, reflect, realign, get input and sharpen your focus. Then re-enter the fray with clarity and precise intent.

If you make this a habit, then you will thrive. When you are thriving, you're having a blast!

3.5
NURTURE RELATIONSHIPS

3.5 A
A WISE MAN TOLD ME THIS TRUTH ABOUT BUSINESS AND LIFE

David Gonski is regularly regarded as one of Australia's most influential people. He is considered a very wise man. So when he laughed out loud at something I'd said, and then gave me a one-sentence, sobering piece of advice, I listened. It's a gem – and vital in business.

Let me be clear. I don't know David Gonski. I did manage to get a meeting with him once, where we sought his support in referring clients to our fledgling business. To his credit and our deep gratitude, he did exactly that.

A corporate shareholder in my business had just purchased a competitor of ours. I was still upset about it, believing this broke an agreement we had with the then CEO not to invest in competitors to my business. I told Gonski this. That's when he laughed, and gave the advice that resonates still today.

Staying pissed off is a luxury in business.

I listened. I had to. It was David Gonski saying it for heaven's sake. Most of all, I reflected upon it. Still do. Over the years the wisdom in it resounds.

Of course things will happen that upset us in business. People quit for a competitor, steal a client or person or two, someone breaks their word, lets you down, or lets themself down. You feel hard done by, betrayed, disrespected or damaged. Egos get hurt. Business can suffer for a while.

The trick is not to brood on it.

Resentment, it is said, is like drinking poison and waiting for the other person to die. It does you no good. Self-pity and resentment are among the most toxic of drugs. Let go of something that is draining you. Angst is simply lost energy, and depletes us.

Sometimes someone does something so outrageous you simply cannot forget or forgive. There are exceptions. But Gonski's words are wise. Staying pissed off IS a luxury in business. We all operate in small 'communities'. The people we know will come around again, either as clients or colleagues.

I make it a priority to reconnect with those who have damaged me or, more often, I them. I try to rebuild relationships. Sometimes it does not work out. As you get older you accept not everyone is going to like you. That is okay. Usually, though, good things come from it.

Here's a challenge for you. Who do you have 'bad blood' with in business or in your life? Which of those relationships would be better 'repaired' rather than left as they are? Prioritise them. Take action! Because, quite simply, staying pissed off is a luxury in business (and in life!).

3.5 B
HOW MY SAAB TEACHES US A CRITICAL LESSON

My car buff mates ridicule me. You see, for the past 25 years I have only ever owned Saabs. I've had seven of them. Saab has gone bust, so they laugh even louder. Little do they know that Saab has taught me a critical 'must have' to survive in business. If you don't do this, you will fail – guaranteed.

Saturday night. A brightly lit Japanese restaurant in Jakarta. My colleague was weeping with tears of laughter.

'What are you going to do now that Saab has gone out of business? No more spare parts for you ... hahahaha!'

He rubbed it in by telling me of a *Top Gear* segment on the demise of Saab. He'd send me the link. Watching it an hour later, I realised why I always bought Saabs. It's the same reason why I keep surviving in business. If you don't have this in your armoury, beware. You WILL come a cropper.

Top Gear made this one critical point: *'You don't understand why a Saab costs so much until you crash it'.*

Saab is an incredibly safe car. *'The Saab designers are pathological about safety.'* I knew that. My first Saab, borrowed from my boss, saved me in a massive crash as I raced to a girlfriend's house, desperate not to miss out on her mother's Malay-style curry. Well, that's my recollection of it anyway.

Here's the point. An area of specialisation from my public relations career is crisis management. One of the first and most critical principles of crisis preparedness is this:

You don't make friends in a crisis.

You have to build relationships and what I call 'goodwill equity' BEFORE you have a problem and need help.

This is not about insincere sucking up. It's about knowing who your key stakeholders are. You must make the effort to add value, be collegial and supportive, to keep in touch and be a positive contributor to their roles and lives. You need to genuinely care about them. It takes persistence, attention to detail and consistency.

It's only then, when the proverbial hits the fan, you're desperate for help and you make that phone call, you are likely to get a: *'But of course, I'd be delighted to help. You can rely on me. Take it as done'.*

Like the crash when driving a Saab, it's at that moment you're reminded why you made the effort so consistently over the years. You see, you don't make friends in a crisis.

Postscript

My PR firm's client was in the news. Every day we'd monitor media coverage, and by 8.30am send an email to the client leadership team on highlights. One morning my key client contact called. *'We're firing our CFO, Arthur, at 10am. This will be big news. Please draft a media statement.'* Just after I'd hung up, ping, the daily media monitoring email, prepared by my colleague Dudley, sitting 20 feet away, arrived. Realising CFO Arthur was a recipient of this regular email, I replied: *'Hey Dudley, as of Monday we can delete CFO Arthur: he's getting fired at 10am today'.* And – ping – I sent the email back to Dudley.

Instantly – PING!!! I got an email from my client contact. *'Chris – this is not helpful.'* You guessed it. I had sent my note to Dudley to the entire client leadership team, including CFO Arthur, who, on reading it, would be surprised to learn he was getting fired in an hour or so.

'Fuuuuuuurrrrrrrrrrrrrrrrkkkkkkkkkkkkkkkkk!' I screamed, literally falling backwards out of my chair. I immediately called CFO Arthur's secretary. *'Athena,'* I said, *'I need your ...'* *'Ahh, Chris,'* she interrupted. *'Glad you called. Thank you so much for helping my daughter with that day's work experience at one of your agencies. She loved it. It has helped her think about what she wants to do as a career.'*

'That's a pleasure, Athena. Now I need your ...' *'Oh, and Chris,'* she interrupted again. *'Thank you also for that recipe for your wife's grandmother's Anzac biscuits. They worked beautifully and we sold a lot at our fundraising event.'*

'That's great news, Athena. Now, Athena ... I NEED YOUR HELP, PLEASE!!! Where is CFO Arthur?' I asked. *'In a meeting with the other leaders,'* she replied. *'Where is his mobile phone?'* I panted. *'On my desk, recharging,'* Athena replied.

'Right, this is what I need please. Would you delete the email I just sent him, from his BlackBerry, and from his computer, and ask all the secretaries to the leaders to delete the same off their bosses' emails?' 'Chris,' she replied. *'You can rely on me. It will be MY pleasure. Take it as done.'*

The email got deleted. CFO Arthur got fired with dignity and respect. (He became a very large client at his bigger and better next job, by the way.) The point is, Athena saved the day. Actually, my relationship with Athena saved the day.

You don't make friends in a crisis. You have to build 'goodwill equity' before the proverbial hits the fan.

Build equity with the big and little people along the way. These relationships are the best part of business, and life. The added bonus is, when the inevitable crash comes, just like my darling Saabs, they'll protect you.

3.5 C
WHY MANGOES ARE A WEAPON IN GROWING YOUR BUSINESS

It started when Andrew Parker sent me a dozen mangoes and a bottle of French champagne.

With that gesture I learnt the secret to guaranteeing referrals and new revenue to my fledgling consulting firm. It's not just relevant to business. It's also a message for life. Make it a habit, always.

When I started my own firm, I had 17 years of 'sweat equity' behind me, of relationships and favours done. I expected a stream of client referrals, a 'thank you and good luck' gesture from a long list of professional *'I owe yous'*.

It didn't happen.* It surprised me. I learnt it is a rare (and often unexpected) person who makes the effort to refer clients to you. It's in their nature. And they are highly likely to do it again, if made to feel appreciated.

That's where Andrew had it right. His firm, Parker & Partners, was growing fast, helped by referrals from a handful of what Andrew labelled his:

MICRophones: Most Important Client Referrers.

He knew this group was priceless, and he treated it as such. He created his MICRophone program to nurture this group, and to say 'thank you' for a referral, fully and appropriately. The MICRophone program ensured Parker & Partners maintained consistent communication with each referrer. Andrew also added value to their careers through a stream of introductions, events and insights. He made sure this small group (who did not know each other in most cases) felt special, appreciated, valued and loved.

Who are your MICRophones? Who are your most reliable, consistent, important 'supporters'? Make a list. Think about what would be the right 'relationship' strategy with each. Write it down. Set a timetable. Implement it relentlessly. Thank them with flair (and within appropriate parameters) when they refer or help you. Nurture them. They are a rare breed, and the most powerful weapon to growing your business or career.

Why did I get the mangoes and champagne? I'd referred a client to Parker & Partners, of course. So started a wonderful experience being part of his MICRophone program. He is still helping me out years later now that he's a senior executive in the airline industry!

Some big exceptions: Savage & Horrigan did receive much appreciated early referrals from people we had just met – Andrew Kitchen, David Gonski, Geoff Levy and others. Also, from established business friends: Jill Craig and Mark Dorney were exceptional. My business partner Jennifer Horrigan's extensive community of investment banking contacts were also constantly generous with referrals from the start. Thank you all!

3.5 D
TOP 10 TIPS TO BUILDING POWERFUL INFLUENCE

What is the most valuable gift the influential people in your life have given you? What made all the difference? Here's the answer. It is the route to building deep influence.

Our 'footprint of influence' is a hard-to-describe ability to be thought of as someone of substance and genuine credential. When you have it, people reach out to you for counsel. You are wanted and needed.

Here's what the most influential people I know always do. It's more important to building influence than anything else. It's what heavy-duty influential people give you, every time:

The gift of time.

If you want to build influence, forge meaningful relationships, or develop a network you can call upon to help, then be prepared to give others your time and your energy.

I spend several hours a week meeting people who want my advice: clients, colleagues, friends, associates and strangers. It's usually personal – about career issues, relationships, aspects of their lives. Often it's my perceived connections that attract them. That's okay. They want to be listened to and perhaps given a suggestion or two. Sometimes they need an introduction, or some other connection. Often it's just a word of encouragement, a hug, a dose of optimism. Most of all, they want my time.

I give it to them. As often as I can. Even though time is what I have the very least of. Why do I do it? It's a privilege to be trusted and wanted. It's also hugely rewarding to help. And it builds my footprint of influence. It opens doors, brings luck my way and creates opportunity. Makes life more interesting. And meaningful.

And the most influential people to me are those who give me time. Nothing in it for them really. Just positive intent and a willingness to listen, and help. It's powerful. I'd do anything for them.

The most influential people I know in business all have common characteristics. They are the key attributes Dale Carnegie recommends in *How to Win Friends and Influence People.* Terrible title. Great book. Should have been called *How to Get on with People and Get on in Life.* Here are the habits of highly influential people. How do you rate against each?

- Be generous in giving people your time, and energy

- Don't criticise, condemn or complain

- Give honest and sincere appreciation

- Connect people with other people

- Become genuinely interested in other people

- Smile

- Remember that a person's name is to that person the sweetest and most important sound in any language

- Be a good listener – encourage others to talk about themselves

- Talk in terms of the other person's interests

- Make the other person feel important – and do it sincerely.

Building influence by giving people quality, no-holds-barred, no-agenda time. It's about listening, being 'present' in conversations, asking questions, making suggestions.

Do that well – consistently – and guess what? You have influence. Give it a go. It works.

3.5 E
A REALITY CHECK FROM AN INDIAN SLUM DWELLER

I am a loner: a shy introvert disguised by an Oscar-worthy extrovert façade. I have few deep friendships (those I have I value greatly), and don't seek out the company of others. I like being by myself. This has never bothered me, until I read this about bamboo. It frightened me. Will it scare you too?

I just read *Behind the Beautiful Forevers*. I did not realise until the author's note at the end that it is a true story, deeply researched. Written by Katherine Boo, it tells of life in a Mumbai slum. It's a confronting story. What scared me was one quiet sentence.

The advice a mother gives her children to illustrate the power of 'communities' supporting each other.

It's easy to break a single bamboo stick, but when you bundle the sticks, you can't even bend them.

Bend one stick of bamboo, and eventually 'snap'. Put huge pressure on a tightly bunched stack of bamboo, and it is unbendable.

I thought about myself as that stick of bamboo. What 'communities' do I have that would gather to protect me if huge pressure came? Who'd step up for me?

That's where I got my big fright. I had to think long and hard beyond family, a small group of work colleagues and valued family friends. I have not done enough to nurture friendships and bonds. It's not a good feeling.

So what to do about it? I am going to start now to put more energy into friendships, and show more gratitude to those who do support me and mine. Also, to make damned sure they know I am part of their 'stack of bamboo'.

Here's my first step. Spend five minutes and do this exercise. I found it difficult. How about you?

QUESTION: Family and relatives aside, who are the five people in the world you MOST like being with?

Make a list of five people now! Why have you chosen them? Are you spending time with them? Do they know how much you like them? Do they know you are in the bamboo stack for them? Would they be for you?

Remember, you don't make friends in a crisis. We must build those relationships and bonds before the pressure comes. I have been selfish and self-centred in my life. It's time to give more of myself, show appreciation and, frankly, show a bit of love. Or I will end up a snapped piece of bamboo. No doubt about it.

Postscript

When I published this story a couple of years ago, I received an avalanche of responses – outraged and irritated friends who told me to 'grow up' and stop seeking pity. *'You're loved, and you know it. You know we'd be there for you, you jerk!'* I was embarrassed. Felt like a bit of a git. But, oh, in truth, it did feel good!

3.5 F
DO NOT LEAVE YOUR JOB WITHOUT READING THIS FIRST

My colleague sat across the table. He'd just resigned. *'I've loved my time here. I want to leave without burning any bridges.'* He then said he wanted to depart very quickly. This would leave his business leaderless, destabilising staff and clients.

He was about to commit a big career stuff-up. Get this wrong, and it haunts forever.

Try to make the grass greener on this side of the fence – to improve your current role – before jumping ship. Sometimes a move is the right step. The trick is to make an elegant exit.

When my colleague said he wanted to depart quickly, I shared this advice from my heart. It's vital for protecting reputations and ensuring we don't burn bridges.

The making of a person is the manner of their leaving.

The way you leave something, whether a relationship or a job, is going to be the most powerful thing you are remembered for. That might seem unfair, but it's reality.

You may have been a great colleague, worked hard and delivered outstanding results. Leave, though, in a poor fashion, and that is what you will be remembered for. It will erode all the good you did and the wonderful goodwill equity you built. Kapow! Gone.

Of course, sometimes circumstances are such that you have no option but to stand up for yourself. That's okay too. Unavoidable.

Think carefully on how to extricate yourself from your current commitments. Manage the process and communication with respect, integrity, candour and sensitivity. Pay real attention to the manner of your leaving.

It is what you will be remembered for. Don't screw it up.

Postscript

Same applies if your 'leaving' is not your decision, but is made for you. I was in Kuala Lumpur on a client issue. My business partner Jennifer Horrigan called. A high-profile client was in crisis. The chairman had effectively fired the CEO – a harsh 'scapegoat' decision following a mistake they had jointly made. The CEO was fronting a media conference in an hour to announce his 'decision to leave'. He was seriously pissed off and was ready to attack the chairman. He'd asked Jennifer to coach him for the media event.

'Crikey! What did you say to him?' I asked. *'I reminded him the way he handled the media event would be how he'd be remembered. It was his legacy. He needed to maintain the high ground: to be relaxed, proud, grateful and gracious. He needed to leave well.'*

That is exactly what he did. He nailed it. Even the chairman thanked him afterwards. And he went on to bigger and better things.

3.6

TAKE
DELIBERATE OXYGEN

3.6 A
WHAT THE FLIGHT ATTENDANT TOLD ME
THAT CHANGED MY LIFE

I love watching safety demonstrations on planes. They always remind me of wonderful advice given by a stranger. It helped change the way I live and work. It will do the same for you.

The flight attendant's name was Christina. She explained that adults should first affix their oxygen masks before helping children with theirs.

'Why should we do that?' I asked her later. Her reply is a message for life.

Take DELIBERATE OXYGEN for yourself. You must be functioning well before you can be at your best for those you love.

This made me realise unless I better managed my stress, I would not have the resilience to keep giving to the people who relied on me. Here's how I am trying to do it:

1. Give yourself permission to take deliberate oxygen, often
Arianna Huffington told us at Cannes: *'We equate relaxation with losers.*

We have to redefine the value of unplugging and recharging. Relaxation is an essential element to creativity.'

Former Wallabies rugby captain John Eales wrote in his *Australian Financial Review* column: *'Sometimes you need to slow down to speed up.'*

I used to feel overwhelming guilt when I'd 'slow down' at work. I'd feel a fraud – as if somehow I was ripping someone off. Now I only feel a semi-fraud when I do it. Progress!

2. Deliberate oxygen as a leadership team

I call them 'fresh air' sessions. We block out two days every quarter if we can. Get out of town. Breathe in the air. Talk. Revisit. Talk about it again with another twist. We always get back to our desks with alignment, clarity and reinvigorated momentum.

Sometimes we run together. We choose a gnarly issue, and talk it through as we jog. The change of scenery clears our heads and helps us nail it. Friend Arvind Singh likes lengthy conversations while walking the suburbs near his Singapore home. The change of scene helps bring him clarity (it makes me sweat a lot!).

3. Deliberate oxygen in your life

You know what does it for you. Fishing. Gardening. Cycling. Reading. Charity work. Whatever it is, stay resilient by keeping yourself 'fit' so as to give others what they need from you.

4. The power of a Third Place

Block a one-hour session weekly to sit in your Third Place (we have home, we have work, and we all need a 'Third Place' where we can be 'still'). Think about your priorities. Are you focusing your time on the right things? Fine-tune your plans. An hour of 'deliberate oxygen' per week will give you clarity, confidence and energy.

You are NOT a loser when you 'unplug and recharge'. You are instead someone committed to doing the best you can for those you care for. I know it's hard to do. For me, anyway. It's critical though. Are you taking enough 'deliberate oxygen' in your life right now?

3.6 B
THE HAPPIEST FOUR HOURS OF MY LIFE

Work had been hectic. Then the Cannes Creativity Festival. Packed days. Then Paris and family. Museums. Galleries. Bistros. Next, Rome, and more of the same. Then we dashed across town to catch the train to Florence. That is when it happened – the screw-up that thrilled my very being. It's a genuine lesson for a happier life.

Back to Rome. We'd crammed into a cab, five of us and about 20 bags. Nosed our way through traffic to the chaotic train station. We had 10 minutes before the Eurail express zoomed to Florence, a 55-minute journey. We bought our tickets and sprinted over several platforms till we reached our train. It departed moments after we had thrown ourselves on board. Problem: wrong train. Going to Florence, yes. But stops all along the way, about 50 of them. A four-and-a-half-hour trip.

I checked my phone. No signal. I looked out of the window. Rolling hills. Villas. Tuscany. No-one could ask me for anything. I had no tasks to do. I had nowhere to go. Could not even think of going anywhere. Just absolute peace. No responsibility. Stunning views. Family. *The International New York Times.*

The tension drained from my body. The next four hours were among the happiest of my life. Seriously.

John Studdert shared a saying with me, told to him by a relative's grandmother. It summed up what happened to me in Rome.

The music is in the silence between the notes.

Some think it a Zen saying, others have attributed it to Mozart, or Debussy.

Nigel Marsh tells a similar story to the one above in his book, *Fit, Fifty and Fired Up*: spending nine hours with wife and four kids stuck in a snowstorm on an English motorway. He loved it!

So, do you ever catch the slow train to Florence?

What do you do to slow down, to celebrate the 'silence between the notes' of life? Not so-called 'work–life balance'. Former Commonwealth Bank CMO Andy Lark puts it this way: *'Don't try to stand in front of the swings and use your BlackBerry. You're going to get hit in the head'.*

True silence. True time to calm yourself, and be absolutely present. Technology off. Pressure off. I've tried meditation, and struggle with it. Alcohol is a temporary fix for me. A poor one. Sometimes jogging helps. Sitting in a beautiful garden can do it. Plane trips are good for this too. In truth, writing is my most powerful oxygen.

They talk a lot about 'living in the moment'. As Mother Theresa said: *'Yesterday is gone. Tomorrow has not come. We have only today. Let us begin.'*

Let's begin. Remember – the music is in the silence between the notes. It really is.

3.6 C
APPLYING THE BRAKE HELPS YOU ACCELERATE YOUR CAREER

I did something really weird in Melbourne today. It's a bit embarrassing. You see, I turned left. It reminded me of the biggest mistake I continue to make. Do you make it too? If 'yes' then STOP! And turn left with me.

The day started early. Emails and calls, even while walking to the six-hour training session I was to lead for 30 up and comers. The session ended, and it was back to urgent emails and phone messages. It was now 4pm. I knew a fast walk would get me back to my hotel in time to put in two more hours attacking my to-do list before a client dinner. I started walking. Then it happened.

I turned left.

Instead of crossing the bridge to my hotel, I turned left into the Victorian art gallery. Not sure why. Just did. Moments later I was in stillness, looking at Picasso, Monet, Turner and the Orientalists. I spent half an hour in the bookshop there, bought pencils and cards, and a book on line drawing. I turned left for an hour. Its impact was profound. Here's why.

Sometimes you have to slow down to speed up.

One hour spent turning left gave me clarity, and inspiration.

My mind settled. The daily dust on my soul was literally washed away. I was transported to another world, of focus and presence, of ideas and courage, of 'pirates' and trailblazers. It reminded me about the 'bigger picture', the richness and vibrancy of the world, and the opportunities in it for me and mine. It reminded me that the angst of business is mainly inconsequential.

I ended that hour refreshed. My mind so much clearer, about myriad decisions and issues. And about some more profound feelings. Can't explain this well. I just loved it. The endorphins were flowing – just as if I'd done a 10km run or eaten a mightily hot curry (the latter more likely in my case, sadly).

Now – truisms are truisms because they are fricking TRUE! *'Can't see the wood for the trees.' 'Wake up and smell the coffee!'* So here's another: *'Sometimes you need to slow down to speed up'.*

Absolutely take yourself seriously, be a 100 percenter, read the blogs, become a thought leader, build 'Brand You', attend the talk, 'turn up' when others just can't be bothered, push yourself to be the very best you can be.

But make sure you also do what I don't do enough of. Slow down, often. Just for an hour. By doing so, you'll be able to more easily speed up along the path you want to go. It doesn't have to be a week on top of Mount Baldy meditating. It doesn't need to be an art gallery. You decide the best 'left turns' for you. But do it, often. Relaxation is not for losers.

3.6 D
DO THIS ALONE – AND IT'S NO FANTASY

A movie on a flight from New Zealand reminded me of something I am simply not doing enough of. I need it. I want it. It is all around me. When I do it, it energises me. What about you? Do you need more of this too?

Night Train to Lisbon, based on Pascal Mercier's book, tells of an ageing, divorced and bored Swiss classics teacher who stops a young woman from throwing herself off a bridge. She is grateful, then runs away, leaving her jacket with him. In the pocket, a memoir of a Portuguese doctor from the 1970s, and a ticket for the night train to Lisbon, departing in 15 minutes. He rushes to the train station in a vain attempt to find the girl. Instead, as the train departs for Lisbon, he impulsively climbs on board.

That is what I am not getting enough of in my life. It is there for all of us. In the words of author Mercier:

Imagination is our last sanctuary.

It's the fantasy of doing something so radical: walking out of my reality into something so different and unknown – that's what seduces me. (I love my reality – and would not trade [most of] it for anything. Just go with the idea!)

Andrew Denton is *'a great believer in daydreaming'.* He talks about learning to do nothing. Daydreaming is in his experience the most fertile creative state there is. *'The simple act of allowing your brain to freewheel can lead you to connections and solutions that have previously been hidden in plain sight.'* We must disconnect to find our own voices again.

Some of the best ideas as part of leadership teams have come from allowing ourselves to daydream: while jogging together, having a sundowner on a river as dusk descends on an Asian city, or walking on a beach at one of our 'fresh air' sessions. (This is where we force ourselves to get out of town to spend a day and a night just talking.)

It's an idea stolen from Tony Blair. In his autobiography, he tells how he and Gordon Brown would fly to New York every few months. They'd book into a hotel, and walk the streets of Manhattan for a day or so, totally anonymously, just talking – about issues, ideas, possibilities. Daydreaming.

Night Train to Lisbon really struck a chord with me. It made my heart skip a beat.

Leonard Cohen's 'In my Secret Life' immediately ignites daydreaming for me. The intent is summed up in this verse:

'I'll be moving through the morning,
Moving through the night.
Moving across the borders,
Of my secret life.'

Spend more time daydreaming. Nurture the secret life within your imagination. Do it for your business, and yourself. No-one will know what goes on there. Unless you want them to.

3.7
GRATEFULNESS/JOY

3.7 A
YOU'LL THANK ME FOR THIS TIP – PROMISE!

I'm in Phuket, and I'm a bit disappointed.

I have been here four times previously, but not for almost 20 years. Until this business trip brought me here. Phuket has changed, for the worse. Overdeveloped, dirty, crowded. I'm sure there are still really good bits. I just did not see them.

I cheered up when I thought about how fortunate I am to have been here many times before, filled with laughter, sunshine and fun. I took those memories with me on the quiet 10 minutes I spent with myself just after I woke up. It's a daily habit I hope you can embrace. This is what I did, and why I encourage you to give it a go too.

I spent 10 minutes 'being grateful' for the great things I have in my life.

Stay calm! Don't stop reading. I have not gone all herbal, burning incense and stuff like that. This is good stuff. Spending time 'being grateful' is like injecting yourself with a dose of optimism and goodwill.

Here's how it works. Before your day gets its momentum and you are lost in busyness, pause. Sit and reflect – for 10 minutes – about the great things you have in your life. This morning, I reflected upon:

- my health, fitness and wellbeing – it's better than it's been in 20 years

- my family – well, safe, secure; I am excited for them and what the future holds (fingers crossed)

- my mother – happily visiting family in South Africa

- the opportunity I have to travel to interesting places, like Phuket. I don't take it for granted

- the fact I have had a life filled with exciting relationships

- my opportunity in an hour to present to 20 senior business people

- my good fortune at 5.30 tonight to run along a beach and watch the sunset.

That took 10 minutes. I finished with a lighter, hope-filled heart, a spring in my step, a recharged resolve to tackle the expectations of me and handle the issues and irritations the next 15 hours will bring.

For some, this 10-minute reflection would lead to a sense of gratitude to a higher being. For me, it's simply a time to quietly reflect that I am lucky indeed and must remind myself of that every single day.

As Brené Brown wrote: *'Joy comes from gratefulness.'* Give it a go. It helps.

3.7 B
FISH AND CHIPS AND THE SECRET TO SUCCESS

I just watched a movie where the lead actor gave me the answer to what 'success' really means. It nailed it for me.

I have been panicked lately by a lack of clarity around what 'success' means to me. I know it's not about having more stuff, or money, friends, power, status. Maybe it's about making a positive difference: in leaving a lasting, meaningful legacy? Or is it in achieving one's potential? It has been causing me anxiety.

Sven Baker recommended I watch *Papadopoulos & Sons*. It was playing on my plane to Bangkok. I watched it. *'So, how do you define success?'* the liquidator asked the failed business tycoon, who had lost his money and returned to work in his brother's fish and chip shop. His answer:

Success is the amount of joy you feel in your life.

Think about it a moment. How brilliant is that! It's not what we have, but what we enjoy, that constitutes our abundance.

'Joy,' writes Zadie Smith in *The New York Review of Books*, *'is different from pleasure.'*

Pleasure is something we can experience a little of every day. I get pleasure out of driving my convertible car with the roof down, from a sunset, a fine wine, a great cigar.

Joy is far rarer. The trick, Zadie writes, is *'to learn to recognise and savour it'*.

In the past few months, I can think of several times when I experienced genuine joy. Walking with loved ones through a shopping centre just prior to Christmas, the holidays beginning, the ability to shop and enjoy, and the laughter of my most precious people right beside me. Or dancing to Madonna's 'Like a Prayer', a few reds under the belt – at the wedding of the son of close friends in a French mountain-top village. And after a week of close nursing at my home, observing my 85-year-old mother regain strength and optimism following a debilitating operation.

I realised my life is sprinkled with moments of joy. These come from a mix of the broad palate of my energies – learning and growing, achieving, generating income and the experiences and opportunity that enables, making a difference, having options, being more in control of my time, pouring out love, being present in those special moments that often slip by unnoticed.

Try hard to recognise where you get your JOY from. Then be clear on what you need to do to create more of it.

3.7 C
HAPPIER AND MORE SUCCESSFUL LIVES – HERE'S HOW

I don't have many regrets, but there are a few. Not having travelled as a young man. Not going to a co-educational school (I have always been shy with women as a result). Not visiting my aged Uncle Ernie in Sussex when I instead flew home to chase a burlesque dancer. Most of all, I regret not having heard this advice 20 years ago.

Forgive my crassness, but it is true. In my early days, success to me was all about chasing women (and catching them!), making money, sports cars, getting promoted and gaining 'power'. I struggled to be happy, always wanting more: striving for something just beyond my reach. Then I wised up. I now view success in a very different way.

I was fortunate to receive a valuable new guiding message when listening to the keynote speaker at a conference I was presenting at in Africa. Here is what that major business icon said:

The most important things in life can't be measured and can't be bought.

Pretty profound! Well, it was to me anyway, and stays in my thoughts daily.

I now realise, as Greek philosopher Epicurus said, *'Nothing is enough for the man to whom enough is too little'.* I need to get clear on what those really important things are in my life. And to savour them.

I continue to spend a lot of time thinking about what success means to me. My assessment evolves. Now it's about my family – their security and wellbeing. My parenting abilities. A solid marriage. Loving relationships. Making a difference. Better managing my fear and the demons in my head. Continuing to learn and grow. Being able to increasingly self-determine what I spend my time on. It's about allowing myself to be happy, now. That's what comes to mind as I write this.

Doug Smollan recommends *True Success,* by Tom Morris. In it, Morris writes about the seven conditions of success. The first is about needing a clear conception of what we want, a vivid vision, a goal or set of goals powerfully imagined.

Start by examining your life. As Socrates said: *'The unexamined life is not worth living.'* Then again, I am a great believer that: *'The unlived life is not worth examining!'*

- Write down all the things you don't like about your life right now (things to change).

- Write down all the things you do like about your life right now (things to preserve).

Then start eradicating (where feasible) the stuff you don't like. And do more of the stuff you like.

Old cliché, but a goodie. *'We only hit what we aim for.'* Therefore, we'd better aim at something high!

'The most important things in life can't be measured and can't be bought.' Please, always remember these insightful words. Are you clear on what the most important things in life are for you? Get clarity. Savour them. Be grateful for what you have. Allow yourself to be happy – now!

3.7 D
A SHORT, SHARP STORY THAT WILL GIVE YOU STRENGTH – GUARANTEED

I was at the junior rugby club ball, chatting to a mother of one of the boys about young girls and first dates. She told me a story that surprised me. It's a message for our lives, and business success. At the very least, it will make you pause and reflect.

Liverpool Football Club toured Asia and Australia recently and the YouTube video of the packed grounds in Jakarta and Melbourne roaring out the club song is amazing: *'YOU'LL NEVER WALK ALONE!!!!!!!!!!!'* It reminded me of what Sophie told me at the rugby dinner.

'When a boy asked me out, my father would insist they pick me up from home and meet the family,' Sophie told me. *'Why did he insist on that?'* I asked. Her answer is the key to giving yourself strength, whenever you need it. Her father's view about the would-be beaus was this:

They need to know who stands behind you.

All of us have certain people who 'stand behind us': who will be there when we need it, who throw their weight and essence behind who we are, who are part of our offer.

We all have our 'rocks'. In business, they might be peers, bosses, mentors, partner companies.

In life, well – we all know who stands behind us. Or do we? We have family and, in my case, a small group of friends, and then maybe one or two surprising rocks who would be there if needed.

Do you know who stands behind you? Do you appreciate it? Do they know you appreciate it? Do you know who you stand behind? Do they know it?

Remember: *'You'll never walk alone.'* Be clear who will be walking beside you. Keep them close to your heart. Let them know you appreciate them. Don't take them for granted. And make sure those you will walk alongside know you are there for them.

Postscript

I quit my lucrative job a couple of weeks ago. Even though I had planned my exit carefully, it was still a shock to me when I resigned. As is common in my industry, and as anticipated, I was immediately sent on 'gardening leave', to sit out my notice period at home. Despite all my planning, I nevertheless felt disempowered, lost, frightened. Then the phone began to ring.

'Come over for a cigar and beer! I am so excited for you.' 'Let's have coffee. I have ideas for you.' 'Join me for lunch. Let's chat about how I can help you with your plans.' Here's the thing. The calls were not all from the people I'd expected. Many of those were strangely silent. I learnt who stood behind me. I will never forget it. They gave me heart when I needed it most.

3.8
SENSE OF PURPOSE

3.8 A
LADY GAGA TAUGHT ME SOMETHING I NEVER DREAMT OF

I'm en route to Los Angeles to give a presentation of *Possums* highlights to a major client conference. The in-flight entertainment has a profile on Lady Gaga. Impressive woman! Gaga said one thing so important I need to share it with you NOW. It actually depressed me. How does it make you feel?

Perez Hilton is a bit of an odd cove. He sure does get access to the stars though. His profile of Lady Gaga was revealing. Gaga is clearly a genuine superstar talent. And smart. In many ways, a positive role model. Something she said got me thinking – and made me sad.

In fact, Gaga's insight built perfectly on a digital campaign I saw, created for Johnnie Walker whisky in China, based around this frightening concept:

Are we a generation without dreams?

Okay, the campaign was not targeting my generation. Nevertheless, it led me to think about my own life, and my own dreams.

I was saddened to realise I don't really have dreams any more. I have goals. Lots of them. For many different aspects of my life. They say without having goals, it's difficult to score. But I don't have a 'dream' any more. My greatest wish and desire is for my children to outlive me. Understandable, but hardly inspiring.

I (sadly) no longer suffer the malaise of youth, as described by Barnaby Conrad in *Fun While it Lasted*. Conrad quotes a French saying: *'I wasn't sure what it was I wanted, but I knew I wanted it very much'.* That's what I want. That feeling. Again.

This is what Lady Gaga had to say: *'I live my life halfway between reality and fantasy. I live in a constant state of evolution, transformation and excitement. I am living my dreams'.* Not exactly her words (I can't be stuffed to watch the show again and be 100% accurate), but that was the thrust of it.

The first of Tom Morris's seven conditions of success is perhaps the starting point of dreaming again:

'We need a clear conception of what we want – a vivid vision: a goal or set of goals powerfully imagined.'

A vivid vision – powerfully imagined. A purpose! That's the key. Some feel that your vision of where and who you want to be is the greatest asset you have.

That's what I am doing right now on this flight. Imagining. Vividly. Thinking hard about what my true purpose is. Maybe there's even a hint of that yearning again. Not sure what I am yearning for, but I know I want it very much! Dream on!

3.8 B
MY CHALLENGE TO YOU:
YOUR LIFE IN SIX WORDS – UP FOR IT?

What I want you to do now is a bit freaky. It might confront you. I want you to imagine that you will die in 20 minutes' time. Here's why.

Ernest Hemingway was once challenged to write a book, but only in six words. He did it. *'For sale: baby shoes, never worn.'* That's the power of storytelling. This apparently led a couple of guys who founded *Smith Magazine* to develop the 'six-word memoir' concept: writing your memoirs in just six words.

So, imagine you'll expire (sorry about that) in 20 minutes' time. You pick up a pen to write your life story, your memoirs. You only have six words to do it in. Give it a go. Here's mine.

Rough diamond. Made a positive difference.

Or maybe:

Loved. Laughed. Infuriated. Learnt. Inspired. Contributed.

That's my view of who I am and what my life has been about. That's what I'd like my obituary to read.

I read a great one, in the obituary of Nora Ephron – journalist, novelist, screenwriter (think *Heartburn, When Harry Met Sally, Silkwood*). Asked to write her autobiography in six words, her response was: *'Secret to life: marry an Italian'.* I love that!

So, turn your computer off. Close the door. Think quietly. Doodle. Maybe make a long list of words that describe who you are, what you have done, what you've brought, what your life has been. Then shape your memoir, in six words.

Perhaps it will excite and comfort you. Or will it be a little confronting and eye opening? It might even push you to change your path, so you could write a different memoir when your life does end. Give it a go. I just did, and learnt a lot. Frankly, it gave me some peace.

Postscript

It's not six words, but I really loved Barack Obama's sentiment at Nelson Mandela's memorial service: *'He was a man of honour and imperfection and that's why we learnt so much from him. He makes me want to be a better man'.*

3.8 C
HOW TO LIVE A GOOD LIFE:
YOU WON'T LIKE THE ANSWER

A loved one was being conferred with a master's degree. I sat in the audience filled with awe: proud, and content with life. Then the guest speaker challenged us to answer a seemingly simple question. Her answer shamed me.

I was thrilled to be in the Great Hall of the University of Sydney for the graduation of 150 students.

Then the guest speaker asked: *'What does it take to live a good life?'* She surmised 'living a good life' was different from a happy life, and does not come from university degrees, big careers or 'good works'. Rather, 'living a good life' is built around one thing. I did not like what it said about me.

'Living a good life' comes from the risks we take.

'A good life is built on how often you feel "uncomfortable" in your life. If you're feeling safe and comfortable, then it is time for risk. Small risks. Being uncomfortable leads to adventure and exploration of the unknown. Whatever you do in your lives, please, make sure it is sprinkled with risk taking.'

Not exactly her words. I was scrambling to get my pen to work on the glossy program cover, but you get the picture.

It reminded me of the death three decades ago in Bangkok, during a coup, of Australian war photographer Neil Davis. Davis described his approach to life this way: *'One crowded hour of life is worth more than an eternity without a name'.*

Midnight Oil's 'Power and the Passion' insists: *'It's better to die on your feet than to live on your knees.'* Neil Davis lived a genuinely 'crowded hour' filled with excitement, adventure, inquisitiveness, boldness. Resisting the normal.

Albert Schweitzer – missionary, philosopher and winner of the Nobel Peace Prize – says this: *'The tragedy of a man is what dies inside himself while he still lives'.* How frightening is that?

And I keep thinking of the last words of the deeply flawed giant Cecil Rhodes: *'So little done, so much to do'*.

I live a fortunate life, filled with opportunity, challenge, affirmation, learning, love. I'm grateful for it. It's a big life, in my little world.

But bloody hell, it is a conservative, timid, predictable, risk-averse, conformist, regimented and restricted life. It's rooted in living up to expectations, of protecting 'reputation' and delivering on obligation and responsibility. I choose it. No-one forces me.

I MUST take action. I must live 'one crowded hour'. I MUST. I WILL!!! Is your life 'one crowded hour'? If not, what do you plan to do about it?

Postscript

Two days ago, while editing this story in Paris, I added the Midnight Oil line, having spotted it when listening to the song during a jog. I read the same line in today's *The International New York Times*: *'It may sound a bit pompous, but I prefer to die standing than live on my knees'*. So said *Charlie Hebdo* editor Stéphane Charbonnier, two years ago. Yesterday, he died standing, murdered by terrorists alongside colleagues at the *Charlie Hebdo* massacre in Paris. *Possum suis Charlie.*

3.8 D
A LESSON FROM CALVIN KLEIN TO
HELP YOU ACHIEVE GREAT THINGS

The image of a bronzed Adonis, clad only in white briefs, inspired me. I felt energised. My heart raced. I bet you'll feel the same way when you read why.

The darkened seminar room at the Cannes Creativity Conference was a sanctuary, away from the glare of a brutal six months of relentless pressure. I was depleted, and two days of insights from global thought leaders on 'what's next' had failed to lift my spirits. The global chief creative officer of Calvin Klein took the stage to explain how the company had built a global brand.

She outlined the business's four operating guidelines. Value number 2 grabbed my attention. I just loved it. It was the inspiration I needed to lift my head and say: *'YES! Let's get cracking.'* Here it is:

Dance with controversy.

'If you really want to connect with an audience in a modern, interesting and meaningful way, then say or do something that provokes – something that creates tension and conflict, and thus genuine engagement. You have to be brave enough to do it, and it needs to be constructive and valid. Be prepared to be controversial.'

Not the exact words, but the overall message. I told this story to a potential creative director hire over coffee an hour later. *'Don't be liked,'* he said. *'Be hated or be loved, but you don't want someone to just "like" you.'*

Tom Peters talks about it this way: *'If you want a career on the high seas, don't join the navy – become a pirate instead'.* Avoid becoming just another sailor in the standard white uniform saluting the flag. Instead, fly the skull and crossbones (a friendly, positive, constructive, value-adding skull and crossbones), and laugh into the wind while thumbing your nose at the merchant navy chugging along in your wake.

I counsel clients who want to be 'thought leaders' in their industry and raise their profile in the media: *'It only works if you have a point of view that is going to stand out, grab attention, and engage: you have to be prepared to be controversial'*. A headline of *Dog Bites Man* is invisible. *Man Bites Dog* though ...

Often just telling the truth is enough to dance with controversy. Do you speak with candour? Speaking 'truth without malice' is hard to do. Powerful people do not always want to hear the truth, and won't appreciate being told the realities. They feel powerless, and often want to shoot the messenger. To face reality and speak the truth is to salsa with controversy.

Here's my point. We live in an uncertain world. Uncertainty breeds fear. You can retreat into safe territory. Pause a moment. Think hard about who you really are, what you really feel, what is the best way to make an impact and deliver the value. Sometimes this means taking a risk: being a pirate.

Put on that 'Girl from Ipanema' track, take the hand of controversy and salsa your way into the moonlight. What a way to travel!

3.8 E
REFLECTIONS ON LIFE FROM THE OPERATING TABLE

I'm about to have a part of me removed, surgically, forever and at this very moment. My nerves are pumping. It's helped me crystallise what makes for a flourishing life. It's a new discovery, and feels right.

It's a minor operation in the scheme of things. Gall bladder removal. Never even knew what a gall bladder was, until a few weeks ago. Certainly did not know you can live without it. Well, you can. I hope.

This hospital visit has made me reflect on 'what's it all about?' I have been thinking about what makes a meaningful life, for me. Then I stumbled upon this thought about what makes us flourish in our lives. Not sure where I got it from. Apologies to the author, whom I'd like to acknowledge:

Most people realise they really need to do things for other people.

'There is a deep fear one's life will be lived in vain – without making a contribution, or a benign difference, to the lives of others. Flourishing means getting on with the things that are important for you to do, exercising your capacities, actively trying to "realise" what you care about and bring it into life. But these activities involve anxiety, fear of failure and setbacks, as well as a sense of satisfaction, occasional triumphs and moments of excitement.

'A good life is still a life. It must involve a full share of suffering, loneliness, disappointment and coming to terms with one's own mortality and the deaths of those one loves. To live a life that is good as a life involves all this.'

I hope you found this of value. I did. It is a message that suits my melancholy mood. It makes me think about what 'flourishing' means to me.

It's not about money, though money can help you do some of the things that help you flourish, no doubt. It is about *'getting on with the things that are important for you to do, exercising your capacities, actively trying to "realise" what you care about and bring it into life'.*

Food for thought.

3.9

UNDERSTAND YOURSELF

3.9 A
HOW THE HEADMASTER HELPED ME TO UNDERSTAND MYSELF

It was snowing as I walked to Reverend Johnson's study that night in West Sussex in 1978. As headmaster of our 700-pupil, private boarding school, he was deciding who would be the next school captain. What happened next has stayed with me till this day.

I was a rank outsider to get the school captain gig. I smoked, regularly got caught smuggling in duty-free booze whenever I returned from holiday in South Africa, got busted one night playing strip poker at the local girls' boarding school, and generally broke the rules.

The odds were stacked against me to get the role: it was a highly prized role usually awarded to the squeaky clean toff who ticked all the right boxes. I was stunned when the headmaster said he wanted me for school captain. *'Why me?'* I asked, bewildered. His answer is burnt into my memory.

'Savage – you are a rough diamond. I'd rather have you on my side than against me.'

That's not the point of this story. It's the set-up. You see, the Reverend had a deep ability to understand the essence of a person. In telling me I was a 'rough diamond', he told a truth I have reflected upon and worked with ever since. He helped me learn to do the one thing vital to success:

Understand yourself.

The first step to change is to understand yourself: being self-aware. Harvard Business School professor Bill George in *True North* writes: '*... the essence of a great leader is about being genuine, real and true to who you are*'.

I work on myself as a project; harder than I do on my job. I give myself constant feedback, and put pressure on myself. I have focused on understanding my nature: what drives me, and why I do the things I do. Through this I can better manage myself, and drive change.

I have also come to understand there are big parts of me I struggle to change. For example, I have never respected rank, only ability. This got me into trouble. Even today I will get impertinent, dismissive and emotional when confronted by judgment from sources whose ability on the matter I do not respect. I have to work hard to control myself, and usually fail.

Robin Sharma puts it well: '*Lead yourself first. You can't help others reach their highest potential until you're in the process of reaching for yours*'.

Start with understanding yourself. Even if, as in my case, it's not always pretty!

Postscript

An old story, but a goodie. A frog and a scorpion needed to cross a river. '*Carry me on your back,*' said the scorpion to the frog. '*No way,*' replied the frog. '*You'll sting me.*' '*Are you crazy?*' replied the scorpion. '*If I did that you would die and I would drown.*' So the frog let the scorpion climb on its back, and swam out into the river. Halfway across, the scorpion stings him. '*Why did you do that?*' cried the dying frog, as they both slipped under the water to their deaths. '*It's in my nature,*' replied the scorpion. Know yourself. Know your nature. The good. The great. The really bad.

3.9 B
WHAT THE THERAPIST TOLD ME
WOULD CHANGE MY LIFE

I went to therapy for five years in the mid-1990s. The issues were complex: deep insecurities, lack of self-love, low self-esteem. It was a burden that was ruining my life. One day my therapist shared the clue to shedding the darkness.

I read about *the top five regrets* people on their deathbeds have expressed, as reported by a nurse who helped care for thousands of people approaching their final moments.

When reading the number one regret I was reminded of my therapist's insight from almost 20 years ago. It helped me regain my life and future. Here's what she told me.

'Should' is shit.

'Every time you hear yourself saying "should", stop and think. Whenever someone says you "should" or "should not" be doing something, stop and think. Why? Because, "should is shit".'

The number one regret of people on their deathbed is this: *'I wish I'd had the courage to live a life true to myself, not the life others expected of me'.*

All my life, I have made decisions based on what others wanted of me: what they felt I should do, be, behave, think or feel. I should be more successful, should be thinner, should speak differently, should not take risk, should not think I was good enough, and should not think that girl would like me or, if she did, that she'd stay with me. I should be fearful of this or that or the other. SHOULD, often followed by NOT, ruled and was ruining my life.

I am not alone. That 'number one deathbed regret' suggests the majority of people are in the same boat.

Here's the point. In business, do not be handcuffed by the expectations of others, often expressed as *'the way we have always done things around here'.*

Don't be restricted by the 'should' and 'should not' brigade. Understand yourself. Have courage. Trust your instincts. Back yourself.

At the Cannes Creativity Festival in 2011, award winning agency Taxi talked about its mantra: *'F**k the Past'*. I don't love that, but get the point. Be respectful of achievements of the older tribe and those who came before, but don't be prisoners to what Steve Jobs called the 'dogma' of business. After all, it's said sacred cows make the best hamburgers.

Understand *'SHOULD is shit'*. Catch yourself whenever you say it.

By double checking the 'shoulds' and 'should nots', you will avoid the regret that most plagues those at death's door: *'I wish I'd had the courage to live a life true to myself, not the life others expected of me'*.

3.9 C
DON'T GET EMOTIONAL WHEN YOU READ THIS

I received a brutal email from a colleague. Blistering. Vitriolic even. Anger oozed out. Accusations abounded. My heart sank. I knew what would happen next. The inevitable outcome saddened me.

I once worked with the wise Paul Cocks. I owe him much, and love him dearly. He was an important mentor to me a decade ago. His insight into people is what I remember most. He quickly sized me up as a hothead: someone who would fire up quickly, get emotional, and attack.

His advice, which he gave me many times when he saw steam coming from my ears, was this:

Give it the 24-hour test.

Before reacting and sending that blistering email, sit on responding for 24 hours. Re-read it 24 hours later. Guaranteed, you will be shocked at what you wrote, and change it dramatically.

John Eales wrote: *'Emotions can be your friend or your enemy. They can drive you to glory or to destruction. They can galvanise or confuse you. Fatigue, emotion and greed will cause bad decisions.'* Know it. Watch out for it.

I have learnt it does not need 24 hours to make a better judgment. Two hours is fine. I have trained myself to manage my emotional explosions this way: I like to vent, so I write the response email, with all its harshness and fury, or make notes on what I will say to someone. Expletives abound. This makes me feel better. Then I park it, even for just two hours. That's all it needs for a more measured, sensible, appropriate and smarter response to become apparent.

If I was more able, I'd be more mature in controlling how I respond in the first place. I have not got there yet. I still respond instinctively, usually emotionally. I am, though, much better at understanding myself, managing emotion, pausing before reacting, and making better judgments after that pause.

That's why I was sad when I got my colleague's email. I knew, from the moment he sent it, he was thinking: *'Oh damn: that was not the smartest thing to do. Wish I could withdraw it. I wonder how Chris will react'*. He would have had butterflies in his stomach, anxious about my response. He's too good a guy to have to feel that way.

I delayed responding. He wrote again a few hours later, apologising and putting his frame of mind in perspective. My heart was with him. I knew how he felt. I have been there many times before.

Far fewer times though since Paul told me a decade ago to *'give it the 24-hour test'*. It's made my life easier, not having to nervously await responses to emails I wish I'd never sent. Give it a go. It helps.

3.9 D
WHAT FOUR BRAVE PEOPLE TOLD ME THIS WEEK

Three men. One woman. Separately. Talking to me over coffee tables. Each did something inspiring. Surprising. Their actions oozed courage, epitomising a habit critical to coping in tough times.

Four conversations. They each told me of something causing them sadness, pain, anxiety, stress, fear. I was privileged. They exposed vulnerability. And, I know, felt better and stronger for having talked about it. Here's the point. It's something I am getting better at doing, and encourage anyone who will listen to do so as well.

It's a good thing to reflect on what makes us anxious and sad – to dwell on it for a while, understand it, respect it, adapt to it.

One conversation was with a long-time business associate and friend. He was struggling. He was saddened, hurt and confused by changes affecting his job and life. I listened, counselled as best I could and suggested others more qualified to help. He needed guidance from me less than an ear to hear his story. Having got it out into the open, he felt refreshed, recharged, lighter, and left the meeting with a sense of energy and optimism.

I reckon it is constructive to sit a while with the melancholy we might feel. Accept the feeling, and to try to understand it. Have the courage to connect with the anxiety or sadness that might be within us. It's also powerful to **TALK TO OTHERS** about what is hurting. Have the courage to share your feelings.

Business IS tough. Our roles ARE getting harder. Pressure DOES keep rising. Demands ARE accelerating. We have a responsibility to acknowledge this, and help ourselves and others cope. Accept that pressure 'gets us down'. We can't be 'up' all the time.

I was taken by this comment by former Australian prime minister Paul Keating, though I recognise it has dangers within it. *'There is a place for sadness and melancholy in life. We don't always want to be sparkling and happy all the time. You need the inner life. The inner sadness which rounds you out.'* I get that. I empathise. I want that as part of me. But it needs a very careful watch-out. I have found talking to others about that inner sadness and anxiety really helps, and keeps me on track. How about you? (If you don't know that right person to speak with, or have a serious issue to discuss and want help, don't forget www.beyondblue.org.au.)

Recognise and respect your anxiety and sadness when it bubbles within you. Don't bottle it up. Have the courage to talk about it with someone you trust. Acknowledge it. Work with it. Manage it.

3.9 E
FALLING IN LOVE WITH YOUR JOB AGAIN

I have discovered how to make sure your job is filled with great moments, experiences and buzz. It also prevents staleness, stagnation and depletion. Seriously: they should make a movie about it.

I got the clue watching *The Grand Budapest Hotel.* The aged hotel owner, who occasionally returns to the hotel where he started out as a bell boy, always stays in the smallest room, with no bathroom. Later, in the flashbacks, we see it's the room he lived in as a young lad, when he was learning the trade, and having a blast. That reminded me of *Citizen Kane*, where the defeated, miserable, sad media tycoon, on his deathbed, murmurs *'Rosebud, Rosebud...'* The camera takes us to the attic of his house where we discover the name of his childhood sleigh was just that.

You see, both depleted men returned to the source of their greatest happiness. They wanted to spend time in that memory again. Here's the insight:

What are your fondest memories so far from you career? Why?

I thought about my *Rosebud* career moments, those experiences that stick out as the most special, fun, inspiring, energising, memorable and meaningful.

Here's the magic. Every one of them related to doing exciting, daring, worthwhile work with clients. It's the client relationships that have given me the biggest buzz.

Des on Lend Lease over 25 years ago, Simon on New Clicks Holdings/Priceline, Ian on the gold mines and tailings dam spills in far-flung countries, Ekkehard 30 years ago through Asia on the Roche Vitamin Information Bureau, Cameron and NutraSweet back in the late 80s, Grant and the Becel days at Unilever, Alan and the Xbox adventure, Gary and his early CEO days at SFG. The list goes on.

To get new *Rosebud* experiences, I simply HAVE to stay on client challenges, in the trenches, delivering the work, creating the value and building the bonds.

Nothing beats it. If you want to be in a service industry, then make sure you LOVE delivering outstanding client service. As Harold Burson, founder of Burson-Marsteller, told me 25 years ago: *'When someone hits my client with an ice pick, I bleed'.* A bit out there, but I get it, believe it, thirst for it.

Think about your career. What have been the moments most memorable to you, where you got the greatest buzz, energy, pleasure, pride, meaning. Are you spending time today on the stuff that has given you the *Rosebud* moments in the past? If YES, delete and move on: there's nothing to see here. If NO, then good for you: you have an opportunity to fall in love again with your career.

Don't waste it. Chase the opportunities to spend time doing what you really love. No-one can ever take those moments away from you.

3.9 F
IF YOU WANT TO THRIVE, ASK YOURSELF THIS

Here's a very personal question. It's likely the first time you'll really think about this. The answer might surprise you, and can energise your future.

Inspiration comes from 'getting started'. If we get cracking on a project, even if we don't feel like it, then very quickly the ideas, momentum and inspiration will come. Environments can inspire (for me, say, Rome, or the artefacts and furniture in my office), but it's taking action that really counts.

Then colleague Neil generously shared a profound insight. This is part of what he wrote to me. *'To be inspired is to "breathe in". There's also nothing wrong with surrounding yourself with the things, and especially people, who give you heart, even comfort.'* In that statement is THE question to answer if you want to thrive. Here it is.

Who are the people in your life who give you heart?

His wise counsel came at a time when I had been searching for 'heart'. Not sure why. My shoulders have been slumped, the cloud a little heavy.

'To give you heart' means to lift your spirits, to put a spring in your step, to give you courage, resolve, fortitude. To make you feel safe, excited, hopeful. Optimistic. 'To give someone heart' is not just about 'inspiring'. It's more gentle, yet powerful. It makes you feel a sense of adventure, self-belief, a desire to flirt with uncertainty. You feel invincible, just for a few moments.

So, here are three important questions if, like me, you could do with help to give you a little heart from time to time:

1. *Who gives you heart?* Who are the people in your life who make you feel the way I describe? When you are with them, you feel energised, your heart lifts, your eyes rise, shoulders back, onwards!

2. *Who depletes you?* Who actually drains you, depletes you, sucks the energy and optimism out of you? The takers. They don't mean to. It just happens. That's the dynamic between you two.

3. *How do you spend more time with the energisers, less with the depleters?* Often the depleters are people we love, who need us, who we want to give to. That's okay. Maybe some of them don't need as much time from you. And maybe you need to spend more time with those rare, special individuals who give you heart.

I was sharing this concept at dinner, and I could see my colleagues asking themselves: *'So, am I an energiser or a depleter?'* Stay calm! We all have relationships that neither deplete nor energise. They are just healthy, genuine relationships. We can all be energising and depleting ourselves. So be it. I am focusing here on the extremes. Consistent depleters. Special energisers.

So, who gives you heart? Are you seeing enough of them?

Postscript

Vale Neil Lawrence, a great mentor and inspiration to many in the Australian advertising and business community. Neil died in July 2015 while holidaying in the Maldives. He was someone who gave me heart. I'll miss him always.

3.9 G
WHY WE ARE ALL TRICKY CHARACTERS

I'm a thief. I claim credit for things I have not done, I lie, harbour resentments, and I'm easy prey to addictions (smoking the worst). I tell you this because I want you to be brutally honest with yourself. Are you brave enough to do it?

If you want to make a Greek misty eyed, just say: *philotimo*. It's a powerfully evocative yet subtle word, symbolising courage, generosity, duty, honour, empathy, humility. It derives from *filos*, friend, and *timi,* honour. It's about giving to others without wanting anything back for yourself, except perhaps love and appreciation.

I'm not Greek. Sometimes I wish I was. Philotimo is a way of behaving which I have struggled all my life to evolve and build in to my nature. We call it 'character'. It's the essence of who we are. Here's how you can constantly 'check in' with what your true character is, at this very moment in your life:

You know what your real character is by what you do when nobody's watching.

That's frightening. I know what I do when nobody's watching. It's not always pretty. I steal things from hotel rooms. I am always looking for praise. If you ever see me at an all-you-can-eat buffet, please, look away. I am jealous and envious. There is also good stuff. And there is good news.

Character evolves over lifetimes. Just as values evolve. It's a constant work in progress. *'Character is the mask left on you by life, and the mark we leave on life.'* Observe yourself develop your character over the years. Work to change what you don't like. Nurture and strengthen what you do.

Don't confuse character with reputation. They are different.

Reputation is what others say of you. You actually can't control that. Character is who you really are. It's within your control. Character is like a tree and reputation is like a shadow. The shadow is what you think of it. But the tree is the real thing.

Civic leader John Gardner, speaking to the Stanford Alumni Association 61 years after graduating, puts it this way: *'You find the world loves talent, but pays off on character.'*

Character is action. Character is destiny.

Character is your personal integrity, without which it is impossible to be honest with ourselves. Vince Lombardi, former coach of the Green Bay Packers: *'From self-knowledge we develop character and integrity. And from character and integrity comes leadership.'* Integrity is a centrepiece of our capacity for happiness. It begins with humility.

'It's your life, but only if you make it so. The standards by which you live must be your own standards, your own values, your own convictions in regard to what is right and wrong, what is true and false, what is important and what is trivial. When you adopt the standards and the values of someone else or a community or a pressure group, you surrender your own integrity. You become, to the extent of your surrender, less of a human being.'

Know yourself. Observe yourself. Forgive the weaknesses and ugly bits. Ease them away. Embrace your positive intent: the evolving values you admire in yourself. Strengthen them. It really is a life's journey. And you know what? It is pretty damned fascinating. Pay attention! It's worth it.

3.10
PUT PRESSURE ON YOURSELF

3.10 A
ACHIEVE OUTSTANDING RESULTS – ON TIME, EVERY TIME

Tony Blair's autobiography was a dull read. But, I learnt a lot from it, only realising its impact some time after I finished it. The gem was in the process he drove to bring peace to Northern Ireland. I immediately stole it, and use it every day to achieve more.

It's vital for business success, and to create sustainable momentum.

Always set deadlines.

There is huge power in deadlines. Putting a flag in the ground and getting commitment from all that *'By [date], we will have taken the first five steps in our action plan'*. Or *'Let's meet again on the [date] and confirm we have achieved a, b, and c'*.

I live now by deadlines. I set them for myself, for leadership teams, around almost everything we do.

When we need to make fast progress against a pressing issue, we create a 30-day plan, and meet every 10 days to update on progress. We regroup on day 30 to see if we achieved our goals. Sometimes it's a 10-day plan, or a 100-day plan. All with agreed outcomes, actions, responsibilities and 'check-in' dates. Sometimes it's simply '10am Tuesday'.

There is nowhere to hide. No escape.

To create momentum, put yourself under pressure. Agreed deadlines are a sure-fire way to do just that. They provide a clear timetable, clarity, sense of urgency and, importantly, accountability.

Before you know it, the job's done, and on to the next challenge. Try setting deadlines for the next 30 days. I bet you never stop doing it!

3.10 B
PRACTISE THIS TO THRIVE – PROMISE!

My doctor told me to lose 20 kilograms. Do you know what I did? I immediately changed doctors! Not really. What I actually did was buy a book by fitness guru Michelle Bridges. In it I found a massive truth. Life changing.

Australian cricket legend Steve Waugh was having his first 'net' practice session as a teenager with the Australian squad. Coach Bobby Simpson watched him smash the ball at every opportunity with youthful aggression.

'You'll never make it as a top-level Test batsmen playing like that,' he told a shocked Waugh. *'But I wouldn't bat like that during a real game,'* replied Waugh. Simpson's reply changed Waugh's destiny. This is what he said:

You do what you practise.

If Waugh's habit was to smash the ball during practice, that's what he'd do in a game. And he would fail.

Mike Arthur puts it this way: *'Unless you practise the skill you want to exhibit, you will never achieve the heights that you dream of'*.

What does that story, about *'you do what you practise',* have to do with Michelle Bridges and her *'massive truth'* advice? Simply this. Her first piece of advice is: *'Break old habits with new habits'*.

If you want to drive change for yourself, think hard about your habits, identify the 'bad' ones, and change them. Waugh immediately stopped playing recklessly in net practice. He formed a new habit of batting at every session *'like in a Test match'*. (I showed my 11-year-old mate the statue of Steve Waugh outside the Sydney Cricket Ground the other day. Point made.)

Catherine Armitage in *The Sydney Morning Herald*: *'Habits are the brain's way of taking a rest. They save us from having to make decisions about every little thing.'*

A challenge for you (and me):

1. For the next week, pay attention to what you do and how you operate. What are your regular 'habits'?

2. Make an appointment with yourself – for half an hour

3. Use that half hour to quietly list the habits you have that you'd like to change

4. Make a long list of new habits you'd like to form

5. Identify your top five 'habits to stop' and 'habits to start'

6. Type it up and have the page laminated

7. Stick it up in your shower

8. Read it every morning – and take action – every day.

Make a start. Break old habits with new habits. It works!

3.10 C
MY HEARTFELT ADVICE TO THE GRADUATES ON HOW TO TRIUMPH

'Bring your "A game" when it really counts, Chris,' cautioned my colleague before a critical meeting. He was off track. Adding value is NOT about nailing big moments. THIS is what REALLY counts.

I had been working on a talk for a group of communications industry graduates, when I chanced upon an article on the greatness of former All Blacks rugby captain Richie McCaw. One sentence summed up the essence of his awesome success. It will form the message of my talk to the graduates. Here it is:

The greatness (of Richie McCaw) is not in the magic of the moment but the ability to repeat what he has been doing game after game ... year after year...

'Not for him the flash of brilliance,' wrote Stuart Barnes. *'His is a case of breakdown after breakdown and contact after contact, collision after collision and victory after victory.'* McCaw just kept on keeping on.

If you want to be 'on the team' all the way to that next World Cup – to be contributing, valuable, wanted, energised – then you must *bring your A game with you every day.*

But wait – there's more. Yes, bring your A game every day. But also do what Richie does so brilliantly – he cheats (now, New Zealanders: calm down Possums, settle, and read on). Barnes continued:

'Richie played his entire career on the thin line between what is and what is not legal. He's the greatest open-side flanker of them all, and the greatest cheat of them all. The latter is a compliment not an insult.'

That's the second message, borrowed from Calvin Klein. First, bring your A game every day. Second, make sure you *dance with controversy.* Flirt with that line between what is 'normal' and what is 'at the edge'. Push it out there. Tom Peters wrote: *'If you want a career on the high seas, don't join the merchant navy. Become a pirate instead.'*

I have worked hard at bringing my A game every day, for 30 years now. I have never rested on my laurels, always judging myself on what I deliver NEXT. I've also loved pushing boundaries along the way. This has not made me universally loved. But it's been huge fun! I want more of it. Some of my mates tell me they want to 'slow down'. I feel exactly the opposite: I want to speed up!

If you want the opportunity of opportunity, bring your A game, every day. Worked for Richie. And I salute him today.

3.10 D
WHERE TO GET THE WORLD'S MOST POTENT APHRODISIAC

'Power is the great aphrodisiac,' Henry Kissinger famously said. Not for me. My constant search, in the first 20 years of my career, for responsibility, control and power never led to any success in that department. What I did get was a brutal lesson about the price of ambition. Pay it with your eyes open.

A young man came to see me. *'I am 24. I want to be a CEO in my industry by age 35. How do I do it?'* My heart sank. I saw myself sitting there, 30 years earlier. Same ambition. I knew why he wanted it, and the price he needed to pay to get there. This is what I told him. It's harsh, but true.

The higher you climb the ladder, the better the view. But, the air is very, very thin.

Climbing the corporate ladder is tough. I know. I have been a CEO consistently for 30 years.

There is a buzz from being in charge. It comes with a price tag. Pressure, stress, long hours. They say it's lonely at the top. You know what? It damned well is.

If you're hell bent on the path to senior leadership gigs, here are four tips on how to do it. Brian Tracy's *Earn What You're Really Worth* helped pinpoint so well what I know in my heart.

1. *Become brilliant at solving problems:* Leadership is about solving problems. It comes with the territory. Almost everything I do, every day, is about a problem. As you get bigger jobs, the problems tend to be the same. The amount of money involved increases. Work on your skills as an awesome problem solver. Keep improving your competencies. Get better and better at the essence of what your role entails.

2. *Work harder (and more effectively) than anyone else:* Face reality. If you want to turbo your career, put in the hard yards. There are

no short cuts. Work two hours more every day than others, then you will rise faster. Be prepared for years of genuinely long, hard, relentless work. Ask any CEO if they made it without doing this. If they say they did, don't believe them.

3. *Push yourself to the front:* 'Continually ask for more responsibility,' Brian Tracy wrote. I have a colleague in Asia. Young, talented, smart, hard working. I started by delegating cautiously to him. He did the work, anticipated, worked long hours, solved problems before I needed to get involved, asked for more rope. We gave it to him. He worked harder. Focused his energies on problem solving. Started to assume more responsibility without asking. We let him do it. He now is doing a role someone with 10 years' more experience should be doing. I expect I'll be working for him soon. That would be fine too.

4. *Work on your 'likeability':* Sounds odd, but it's a factor. Be someone people enjoy being around. Make an effort to be accessible and friendly. Be 'good company' at social events. People do business with people they like. And this applies too to those who are given opportunity. Not always, but it helps!

Become brilliant at solving problems. Work harder (and more effectively) than anyone else. Push yourself to the front. Work on your 'likeability'. But do tread cautiously. Remember what a banker told me (and never fall into this awful trap):

'Success in this business [banking] is like having four hotplates: family, friends, health, success. If you want success, you will only have time to achieve one other hotplate. Which would you choose?' (Reread that – please. Think about it. Carefully. How terrible is that?)

Go hard, be bold, but please, take care of yourself.

3.10 E
WHY IT'S OKAY TO PUT ON A PERFORMANCE

In the past couple of years I have been trying to define my 'purpose': what it is that motivates and drives me, and what is the legacy I want to leave in my little world. I don't have it refined yet, though I'm settling on something like: *'To inspire confidence and hope in those I love and care for'.*

Now, I love and care for a lot of people! It's part of my DNA. And I guess I am thirsty for the love in return.

That's not the point, though. I settled on this 'purpose' because I know I have the power of personality to deliver on it. I am able to 'lift people up'. Not chest beating: it is just reality. (I also have the ability to deplete people, profoundly. But the good stuff just outweighs the bad.)

So, I am able to 'lift people up'. Sometimes I just don't feel like it. I am grumpy, self-centred, irritated. I know my next meeting guest really needs me to deliver 'inspiration'. I just don't want to. I can feel resentful having to do it. It's a selfish feeling. I don't know why I have it, but I do.

That's when I think of Steve Lyons.

Steve was one of the world's great inspirers. His enthusiasm was intense. He lifted you up. Always. Here's the thing. Often Steve would share his abundant enthusiasm and inspiration when his heart simply was not in it: when he was in a dark place. He managed to do it by adopting this golden rule:

Sometimes you have just got to put on a performance.

'Go to the washroom. Look in the mirror. Say to yourself: "Okay, let's get this show on the road", and come into the meeting and perform – deliver the goods.'

Not exactly authentic. Does it matter? Is that wrong? If part of your role and purpose is to keep giving, I reckon it's fine to occasionally *'put on a performance'.*

Done is better than perfect. Go hard! Make people feel great – whenever you can. Even if it means putting pressure on yourself to deliver a performance.

3.11
BE YOUR OWN BEST COACH

3.11 A
A WEIRD STORY ON HOW TO BE YOUR OWN BEST COACH

This story might be just too weird. I'll take the risk, and share an idea at the core of my resilience in my career, and life. Be warned: it's a bit odd.

I worry about ending my career, at a timing not of my choosing, knowing I could have achieved more. Actually, this fear permeates my whole life: will I be the best I can be, as a father, son, husband, brother, uncle, in–law, cousin, friend, boss, colleague, neighbour?

I fear it because I know I am weak and flawed. I live on the edge of a darkness I can easily slip into: not an evil place, just one filled with slovenliness and lost opportunity. '*A tree falls the way it leans. Watch out which way you lean.*' I keep leaning the right way in my life, just, by following three steps, every day. One is really weird.

1. *I treat myself as a project*
   This is not the weird part. That comes later. I work harder on myself than I do on my job. I set personal goals, and work hard to make progress against them. I put pressure on myself, set deadlines and drive myself to do exactly what I say I will do. I don't always succeed (I am flawed and weak, remember), but I try.

2. *I give myself feedback, constantly*
   This isn't the weird bit either. I thrive on giving myself feedback. I critique my every day. What did I do well, what could I have done better, was I appreciative, did I hurt anyone, what more could I have done to prepare? I am brutal in my feedback to myself. My focus is improving my reputation with myself.

3. *(Here's the weird bit) I give that feedback to an 'eight-year-old me'*
   When I give myself feedback, I do it with the vision of me as an eight-year-old boy in my mind. I give the eight-year-old me the feedback honestly and directly, but in a warm, fatherly tone and manner. I say:

   'Chris, my darling: you're a good boy, and I love you. I need you to know you could have handled that meeting today with Dave much better. You frightened him. He did not deserve that. I know you did not mean to, and you wanted to help him. There is a better way you could have done it. Here's how ...'

   I figuratively put my arm around the eight-year-old me, and hug myself every night. *'You're a good fellow with a big heart, Chris. I know you are often scared. It's okay. You're doing well. Yes, you made a couple of mistakes today. You also did a lot right. Well done, darling boy! Learn from those mistakes. Keep backing yourself. I love you. Good night.'*

Weird? Okay, it is. I get that. But I don't care. I reckon we're all eight years old. We want to be loved, have a sense of belonging; to be treated kindly. So treat yourself that way!

I give myself robust feedback. I critique my days and my performance. But I am kind to myself. I forgive my weaknesses, and work gently but firmly to encourage progress.

Leonard Cohen put it so well at his press conference in late 2014 to launch his *Popular Problems* album, two days before his 80th birthday.

'... Acknowledge that everyone suffers, everyone is engaged in an almighty struggle for self-respect, for meaning and significance. The first step would be to redefine that your struggle is the same as everyone else's struggle ... I think that is the beginning of a responsible life.'

'Be kind,' as Philo said, *'because everyone you meet is carrying a heavy burden.'* That includes you. And me.

3.11 B
HOW TO FIND INSPIRATION WHEN YOU NEED IT

I found the answer to what genuinely inspires me when a colleague did not like a suggestion I made. There it was. Right in front of me. Does this hold true for you? Is this a key to your inspiration?

'You must get closer to the client work,' I encouraged my colleague, who spends most of his time 'managing' business issues. He looked uneasy. Silent. *'What's up? Is there a problem with that?'* I asked, perplexed. *'Well,'* he replied hesitantly, *'it's just that ... the client work thing ... it's kind of not what I do these days. I am just not sure I am able to do it any more.'*

There it was. The secret to inspiration. It was clear what my colleague needed to do to revitalise and inspire his pants off. Hold true for you too? Sure does for me:

To thrive, learn what makes you uncomfortable: then attack it – head on.

We often avoid what we need the most.

If we duck and weave away from what makes us uncomfortable, a feeling builds of inadequacy, of being second rate, not good enough, a pretender. It seeps under the skin, and puts doubts into your head. It becomes part of what Buddhists call the 'chattering monkey' that is the mind, our thoughts.

There is another way. It involves being your own very best coach. It needs courage. When you get started, it becomes addictive. Here it is:

1. Write down the stuff that makes you feel uncomfortable. Describe the feeling, and why it makes you feel that way.

2. Then make a plan to push yourself into that 'discomfort zone'. How can you expose yourself to those circumstances over the next few weeks?

3. Take action – schedule it. Make it happen.

When you tackle discomfort, your heart races, endorphins flow, you're alert, on the edge, you feel alive! When you embrace your discomfort zone, your head is held high, shoulders back, spirits soar.

Don't delay. Don't allow yourself to feel second rate. Or end up, like me, with regrets.

Be your own very best coach. There is no growth in your comfort zone. It is not easy. It involves stumbles and setbacks. That's okay. Really it is. You see, struggle is the evidence of progress.

Little steps of progress: big licks of inspiration. All to be found in your discomfort zones. Give it a go! Back yourself. You won't regret it.

3.11 C
SCREAM JUST BEFORE EVERY UNPLEASANT MEETING

Know this feeling? A meeting is approaching you really don't want to do. Every ounce of you is resisting it. Here's the secret to never feeling this way again. Just scream out: *'AEEeeeeeeeeeeeeeeeeeee!!!!'*

Roger is a media industry leader. He was exploring career moves after taking a sabbatical.

As we talked, he told me of a technique to approach meetings or events you are not looking forward to. Whenever you have an appointment approaching you feel flat about, which is causing angst in your gut and a *'bloody hell'* reaction when you think about it, then follow his 'AEE' strategy:

Acceptance, enthusiasm, enjoyment.

Acceptance: Stop resisting the inevitable. Accept you have to turn up to that event. There is no escape. It is going to happen. Get used to the idea. Acceptance.

Enthusiasm: Think about all the things about the event you can enjoy and get positive value out of. *'It's a "must have" meeting and real progress will come out of it.'* *'I will find three things about that person to really like.'* *'I am going to make a real connection with that person.'* *'I am going to meet five people at that cocktail party who I learn something from.'* Get enthusiastic about what you can contribute or gain from that event. Enthusiasm.

Enjoyment: If you stop angsting about the upcoming event and accept it, and instead start focusing with enthusiasm on its potential positive aspects, you'll find you will weirdly enough start to look forward to it. Then, no kidding, you'll actually enjoy it. Enjoyment.

This has been my experience. I have made it a habit to scream *'AEEeeeeeeeeeeeeeeeee'* whenever my heart sinks over an upcoming meeting.

Roger mentioned he'd learnt this approach from *A New Earth* by Eckhart Tolle. I have the book beside my bed. It's not an easy read but I am quietly working my way through it.

Have to go now. Have an appointment with my dentist in an hour. AEEeeeeeeeeeeeeeeee!!!

3.11 D
FOUR HABITS TO KEEP YOU POSITIVE
AND STRONG, EVERY DAY

I get plenty of feedback. Most of it 'constructive': where I must improve, miss the point, need to stop or start doing something. Most of it is fair. Still, it wears you down. I cope with it using these four habits.

I am getting better at embracing feedback, to learn and grow from it. Often, people forget to give you positive reinforcement. They think you don't need it. *'You're a strong person – you can manage. Man up!'* Not true for me.

I need regular positives to keep me strong. If those hugs are not forthcoming, then I give them to myself. This is how I do it. It sustains me, and makes me stronger. First, we have to do this really well:

We have to become our own best coaches.

Here are the four habits I use to 'coach' myself every day:

1. *Be kind to yourself:* Make sure the voices in our heads are kind. Take the feedback. Learn from it. I give myself feedback with humour and kindness. I shake my head at my foibles and weaknesses, forgive myself, and beam at strengths and triumphs. Leonard Cohen again: *'There's a crack in everything, that's how the light gets in.'* It's okay to be flawed. Really. It is.

2. *Be optimistic:* We need to train ourselves to react to what happens to us with an optimistic view: to become outstanding 'disputers of negative thoughts'. When that voice says: *'Hey Chris, you will fail. You are not good enough. You can't make it'*. That's when we need to immediately dispute with: *'Rubbish: of course I can! I am able. I can do it. I will give it a go. It will be fun'*. Rather than 'react' be more measured in the way you 'respond'. There is a difference.

3. *Give yourself opportunities for positive feedback:* I do this through the training I lead. I can see the positive impact on attendees. This

boosts me. I also get reinforcement from my blog. Despite regular feedback slaps, I do get positive feedback from it, in writing and in person. This makes me feel worthy and wanted. I need this for my confidence. So I make sure I get it.

4. *Be grateful:* I have been training myself to be grateful for the good in my life. I was in Singapore, working hard, tired, missing home and worried about stuff. I paused, and reflected on how lucky I am, to have the experiences I am having, the colleagues I have, the challenges in front of me. Being grateful keeps me 'vital and energised'.

What do YOU do to stay positive? Do you hug yourself often enough? Are you your own very best coach?

3.11 E
HOW TO CREATE A HAPPIER, MORE SUCCESSFUL LIFE

This is the most important story I've ever written. Perhaps it shames me. Do you recognise big truths in it for you? It's about the cause of much of my pain, and my greatest enemy. If better controlled, happiness and success are guaranteed.

My 'greatest enemy' is my thoughts. They play havoc with my mind. Once a prisoner to these thoughts, my mind does all it can to strengthen insecurities and doubts. It feeds on putting me down. Arianna Huffington calls it: *'The obnoxious roommate living in our head'*. If you have that roommate too, here's one action you can take to guarantee a happier, more successful future:

Improve your dialogue with yourself.

Even our worst enemies don't talk about us the way we talk to ourselves.

We have to get better at distinguishing between real dangers and the imagined ones our minds conjure up. I get paralysed with catastrophising, believing the worst of me and for me. Most of it is just total crap. A famous deathbed quote: *'There were many terrible things in my life, but most of them never happened'*.

I have taken my inspiration to tackle my mind, and to make it my friend, from 19th century British explorer and pioneer, Edward Eyre (think Eyre Peninsula, Lake Eyre). His family motto: *'If I Can'*. I love that. If I can. Remember this: *'Life's battles don't always go to the strongest, or the fastest man (or woman), but sooner or later the man who wins is the man who thinks he can'*.

Here's the plan. I am the boss of me. I will make my mind my friend. This is how:

1. I will remember I have the power to control my thoughts. Yes – if I can. And I can!

2. I will welcome challenges and obstacles with open arms. Stoic Roman emperor Marcus Aurelius tackled every setback with this frame of mind: *'Welcome! You are here for my benefit! You are the VERY thing I was looking for!'* Everything is the right material to bring out our growth.

3. I will create a visual reminder to help instantly 'switch' me into 'control my mind' mode. It's a wristband I will wear. When I look at it, it immediately says PIE to me.

    - The **P stands for purpose:** it reminds me my purpose is to uplift those I care for with optimism, confidence and hope. That includes myself.

    - The **I stands for inspire:** it reminds me to ensure my thoughts and responses at that moment do all they can to inspire me, and those with me.

    - The **E stands for empower:** it reminds me I am empowered. I am healthy, surrounded by love, have talents and abilities, have options, security and hope. Our outlook on life is a direct reflection on how much we like ourselves.

I am determined to be happy, NOW. I won't allow my mind to stop me from that. The father of positive psychology, Dr Martin Seligman: *'When we take time to notice the things that go right – it means we're getting a lot of little rewards throughout the day.'* I will focus on what I DO have … not on what my mind tells me I don't have or makes me fear losing.

Buddhists talk about 'quieting the chattering monkey'. Tom Morris adds: *'By changing our attitudes we can change our lives. Your life is what your thoughts make it. We need to learn to banish unhelpful doubts.'* Dr Seligman says the happiest people have learnt to control their minds by becoming expert 'disputers' of negative thoughts. They have become 'learned optimists'.

Here's one more concept from *The Fall of the Human Intellect* by A. Parthasarathy. We have the intellect, and we have the mind. *'The human mind can become ruinous if the intellect is not developed enough to govern it. The mind behaves like a child while the intellect plays the role of the adult. So does the mind need the attention and the guidance of your intellect. An uncontrolled mind can wreck a being.'*

Often I observe my mind racing off on a mad course. My intellect steps in: *'Aha! There go those thoughts again. Look how the mind laps them up and thirsts for more. Need to settle this down and get back on track'.* Coach Clare describes it as the elephant and the rider. The mind is the elephant, the rider the intellect. Sometimes the rider just has to hang on and observe as the elephant lumbers through that jungle. Other times, the rider can gently lead the elephant in another direction.

If you are still with me, take a bow. **We have to improve our dialogue with ourselves.** The only way I can do that is to control my thoughts, and my mind, much better. As the Margaret Thatcher character said in *The Iron Lady*:

'Watch your thoughts for they become words.

Watch your words for they become actions.

Watch your actions for they become habits.

Watch your habits for they become your character.

And watch your character for it becomes your destiny!

What we think we become.'

3.11 F
HOW TO USE TOMATOES TO EXPLODE YOUR EFFICIENCY

Here's a simple idea that will make a massive difference to your effectiveness and efficiency. It sounds weird. I tried it. And – it works! It's a 60-second read that will save you many hours of time.

I was preparing for a series of speeches I am giving around Australia. I had at least two hours of hard work to do to update a presentation to make it current and extra valuable. I was struggling to get started. The task felt big. Then I remembered Kuba's weird advice at breakfast two months ago. *'Enjoy tomatoes if you want to turbocharge your effectiveness,'* he'd said. What he meant was this:

Use regular breaks to accelerate your productivity.

Stay with this. It's good stuff.

Kuba shared the Pomodoro Technique with me, a time management method that uses a timer to break down work into intervals traditionally 25 minutes in length, separated by short breaks. These intervals are known as *pomodori*, the plural of the Italian word *pomodoro* for tomato. The method is based on the idea that frequent breaks can improve mental agility.

There are five basic steps to implementing the technique:

- Decide on the task to be done

- Set the pomodoro timer to n minutes (traditionally 25)

- Work on the task until the timer rings

- Take a short break (3–5 minutes)

- After four pomodori, take a longer break (15–30 minutes).

I gave it a go. I started by using the JFDI approach – 'Just Fricking Do It'. Get started on a task but have the deal with yourself that if after 10 minutes you want to stop, you can. At the same time, I set my timer for 25 minutes, and then got stuck in. Suddenly, the buzzer buzzed. Wow. That was 25 minutes? I took a short break. And then went again. Repeated it four times. And I was done. Felt great. Nailed it.

The next day I had to get started on arranging a detailed schedule for a three-day visit to Singapore in a month. It involved making contact with about 20 people, and arranging a range of meetings and events. It felt daunting. So I attacked it with the Pomodoro Technique. I used the first 25 minutes to plan carefully what I wanted to achieve in those three days, and with whom. Then had a short break when the buzzer went. And then spent 25 minutes making contact with all I wanted to meet. Bang. One highly effective hour, including two pomodoros. Big progress made. Onwards.

What did the Daddy Tomato say to Junior Tomato on the family walk? *'Ketchup.'* (With thanks to *Pulp Fiction*). So – want to catch up time and get more done, more effectively? Try the Pomodoro Technique. I like it. Thanks, Kuba!

3.12
TAKE RESPONSIBILITY

3.12 A
A CRITICAL BUSINESS 'MUST DO' –
SHARE IT AT YOUR PERIL

There was a disaster on the mountain K2 a few years back. Many climbers were killed. A survivor outlined his perception of what caused the tragedy. It is a truth that lives every day in our business lives, and beyond. It's not for sharing. You absolutely HAVE to do it alone.

Several groups of climbers, of various nationalities, ended up at the same spot at the same time on the climb to the summit of K2, one of the highest peaks in the world. Huddled together that night, they agreed to continue the last stage to the top as one group. They shared the various responsibilities among the original teams. That sealed their fate. The next day, a series of simple, but sacrosanct mountaineering rules were broken, and many plunged to their deaths. This is what went wrong.

When you share responsibility, you relax.

There was a scenario at work some years ago. We were planning to merge two businesses. My colleague wanted to oversee communicating and managing the changes with one of the businesses. I'd do the other. We'd both supervise. NO FRICKING WAY! One person HAS to be ultimately accountable and responsible, keeping the view across every aspect of the project, living and breathing it, ensuring no stone is left unturned.

By sharing responsibility, critical steps would be missed, inaccurate assumptions made, key conversations not held, and mistakes would inevitably unfold.

It's what happened on K2 that day. Each team assumed the others were ticking boxes on vital steps. They all relaxed. When you relax, it's a ticking time bomb to disaster.

Take responsibility. Make it clear the buck stops with you. Make sure your colleagues know exactly what is expected of them, and what they can expect from you. YOU must take the initiative to lead, to sweat every aspect, to be relentless in ensuring no relaxation.

If you are NOT responsible, clarify up front who is. Ensure alignment on exactly what is expected of your role in the project.

Ensure absolute clarity on expectations, and who is responsible. Then step up and deliver your part.

It's a lesson those climbers learnt that sad day on K2, many paying the ultimate price in the process. Learn from it. Never share responsibility (oh, but always share the credit).

3.12 B
SIMPLE ADVICE FROM A CRUSTY OLD COACH

Sometimes in life a gift comes along exactly when you need it. It happened to me. Out of the blue, I had the answer to guide me out of a terrible funk. I was lost. Then I was told this, and it changed everything.

Six hundred of Sydney's most influential citizens, including cabinet ministers, the mayor, rock stars and sports heroes filled The Star hotel event centre. They were there to help launch the Thomas Kelly Youth Foundation. Thomas died aged 19 on his first night out in Sydney when 'king hit' (or hit by what is now branded, a 'coward's punch') by a drunk, anger-fuelled stranger.

I was distracted, thinking about recent feedback at work that I found unfair and bizarre. It was then cricketer Matthew Hayden spoke. He quoted famed rugby league coach Wayne Bennett. When Matthew had been failing and was dropped from the Australian cricket team, Bennett told him this:

Don't get bitter, get better.

It was the perfect gift. I lifted my head, grabbed a pen, and wrote it down. Don't get bitter, get better.

I did not like the feedback. I thought it was really unfair. From the giver's perspective, they were making a point. I didn't agree. Self-pity and resentment are among the most toxic of drugs. Don't let them seduce you.

As you get older, said civic leader John Gardner in his Stanford Alumni Association address given 61 years after graduating, *'You come to understand that most people are neither for you nor against you, they are thinking about themselves'.*

I have a choice. Get bitter, stew over it, and then try to prove that I am right. Or follow Bennett's wise counsel: take responsibility and focus on getting better. Put all my energies on sharpening, evolving and improving. Get better. And better. Do that, and everyone wins. Particularly me. Don't get bitter, get better.

It changed everything for me in a second. Write it down. Make it your home page. Tweet it. Write it on a wall. Great bumper sticker. Or tattoo. Hmmmmmm. Now, there's an idea ...

3.12 C
HERE'S THE BEST ADVICE YOU WILL GET ALL YEAR

Stretching out before us is the future; winking optimism, opportunity, freshness and renewal. To help make this next 12 months great, I am going to share this brilliant piece of advice. It's a gem.

I love the 'fresh start' January brings. It lifts my spirits, and makes me feel 'anything is possible'. I plan accordingly! Sadly, history tells me by about March, I will have sunk back into the depths of deadlines, to-do lists, pressure and a string of broken promises with myself. I lose sight of what inspires and gives me purpose. Not this year. No, no, no! I am taking full responsibility to ensure this does not happen again.

You see, this advice I know will make this year a triumph of mindfulness and happiness. It can for you too. If you're up for it.

Take more time, cover less ground.

So said writer and mystic Thomas Merton, quoted in Daniel Klein's philosophy on the best path to a happy and fulfilling life, *Travels with Epicurus*. Klein goes on to suggest another powerful habit, which dovetails perfectly with this theme: *'Be clear what gives you pleasure, and do more of it.'*

This is what I plan to do. If I don't force myself to slow down, to pause and reflect, my life flashes past and it becomes a missed opportunity. Sometimes you need to slow down to speed up. I must cover less ground, and do so with more presence, and thoughtfulness. Here's my two-part plan:

1. *Get clarity on what gives me pleasure*
    Are you clear on where you get the most pleasure from in your life? I am clearer today than I was two weeks ago, now that I have really thought about it. It shocked me. My pleasure comes from very simple things: being together with family having a meal somewhere new, walking with my mother and holding her hand, the feeling after a solid run, learning something new, great

conversations, swimming in the ocean, writing, doing something for others (coaching an under-10s rugby team was incredibly rewarding). It's a pretty short list, filled with stuff I simply don't do enough of.

2. *A weekly one-hour 'fresh air' session with myself*
I am now diarising a weekly one-hour meeting with myself, at my Third Place (not work, not home, but somewhere else where I can relax and think). I will use that hour to sharpen clarity on three things:

a) What is most important to me in my life: am I giving those the right focus

b) My 'pleasure' list: am I finding time to sprinkle my weeks with what I get the greatest buzz from

c) What I need to STOP doing: what has crept in to my life that is not productive?

Take more time, cover less ground. Be clear on what gives you pleasure, and do more of it.

I reckon – hand on heart – if we can do this well, our lives will be happier and more fulfilling. Good luck with it. And I do hope a weekly dose of *Wrestling Possums* or half an hour dipping into *Savage Oxygen* makes it onto your 'pleasure list'.

3.12 D
THE OBITUARY YOU NEVER WANT TO HAVE

I am determined to make the year ahead unforgettable: a year I will cherish for the rest of my life. You can too, if you are brave enough to take this one very simple action.

It was the death of former New York State governor Mario Cuomo that sparked me into action. His obituary in *The International New York Times* gave me the clue. *'Cuomo,'* it read, *'may be remembered more for the things he never did than what he accomplished.'*

I'll tell you why they said that of Cuomo shortly. Point is, his is a legacy of missed opportunity, of unrealised promise. Join me in making sure the next year is not one to be remembered for what we did not accomplish. Take responsibility now to make the next 12 months GREAT for you. Start by remembering the words of William Ernest Henley in his poem *Invictus* as you consider your goals and aspirations for the year ahead:

I am the master of my fate, I am the captain of my soul.

Cuomo was at his highest profile when he was considering standing for president, up against Ronald Reagan. He had two chartered airplanes on the tarmac at Albany airport waiting to fly him to New Hampshire to pay the filing fee that would put his name on the state's Democratic primary ballot for president. The world's media watched with bated breath. This was his moment. He never took that plane trip – never stood – and that's what he is most remembered for.

So – make the year ahead one of accomplishment. This is how to do it:

1. Get clear on the one goal you have that, if achieved by a date in the next 12 months, will make the most positive difference to your happiness and life.

2. Write down that goal in the past tense, as if you have achieved it, and then put a date beside it. For example: *'I climbed Mount*

Everest. 15 December' ... 'I got promoted to manager and now run the Western Region. 10 October'.

3. Make a long list of everything you need to do to achieve that goal.

4. Then make a plan. Break all those to-dos into three phases – phase one, two and three. List out the most immediate, say, six to eight priorities in phase one.

Then take the one action I told you would make all the difference:

5. TAKE ACTION! That's it. Take action immediately on your phase one list, and then make sure you take action every day against that list.

Make a start. Get moving. Every step of progress, no matter how small, is to be relished. Soon you will have momentum, and will be accelerating towards success.

Don't let this be a year with a legacy of missed opportunity. You ARE the master of your fate, the captain of your soul.

Pick the goal that will make the biggest difference. Follow my five steps. Persist. DO NOT GIVE UP!

3.12 E
WHAT HAPPENED WHEN THEY FOUND A TUMOUR IN MY THROAT

'Yip, looks like cancer,' the specialist sighed, pointing to the video picture of a tumour growing from my vocal chords. *'Treatable?'* I asked, petrified. *'Oh yes,'* he replied. *'But not necessarily curable.'* This was on a Monday. So began the worst week of my life.

My voice had been getting increasingly hoarse. *'Acid reflux caused by increasing size of your gut,'* the GP counselled. I struggled swallowing; could only speak in a whisper. The specialist had the bedside manner of a cobra; he found a tumour, speculated cancer, and gave zero reassurances.

'I'll remove it surgically on Wednesday. Then pathology. If it's cancer, which it probably is, come to the hospital next Tuesday and we'll advise treatment. If it's early stage, then likely more surgery and radiation. If it spread, then chemotherapy too and a 50/50 survival chance. If it spread a lot, then there's not much we can do'.

I walked into the sunlight, devastated. So began the five worst days of my life, underpinned by one terrible thing:

Uncertainty.

Did I have cancer? What would happen to me next? How quickly would I die if it had gone too far? I know a cancer diagnosis is not always a death sentence, but it's hard not to think the worst. Not knowing was the most debilitating curse. If you have certainty, you can handle it. I needed to wait five days for that.

My reaction to potential throat cancer – and potentially, death

I had no fear about my potential demise. My focus was my children: how to help them cope with the loss of their father. I immediately prepared a clear financial plan for my family. Knowing they would be okay gave me comfort. I worried about how to tell my mother. I kept really busy: threw myself into work; at night, wrote 12 *Possums* posts!

The surgery

Two hours under the knife on the Wednesday. The cobra was concerned that if the tumour was too tightly lodged around the vocal chords, he'd only be able to take samples. *'We need to know if it is a cancer first in that case, to inform how much we need to cut out of the vocal chords.'* All went well. Tumour totally removed except for submerged 'stalk'. *'It's 50/50 cancerous,'* the specialist told us afterwards. *'90% of the tumours I remove from that spot are cancer, but this one looks a little unusual.'*

My realisations as I waited for the results

An overwhelming sense of gratefulness for the life I have had. To die now would be premature, but okay for me. A stark realisation I am a loved person. I am so grateful for that. I work too hard and put too much emphasis on my job and career. I should have enjoyed the spoils more. I have foolishly taken the future for granted. I am a selfish prick – allowing habits of overeating, smoking and drinking. I would have let my family down badly. They need me more than I need me. I failed them. The guilt was overwhelming. *'I am so sorry,'* I kept sobbing to myself.

The pathology results

2pm on Friday the call came in. *'Benign polyp – all clear. I'm surprised. I was sure it was cancer.'*

What happened next

I told my wife. We hugged. We rang our children. They cried. I emailed colleagues. They cheered. I went home.

On my kitchen table that morning I had left two folders. Each represented a very different future. The first, all the details of an exciting trip in a few weeks to Provence to the wedding of the son of great friends. The second, a folder entitled 'Me,' in which were all my worst-case scenario plans, from 'fighting it', to final wishes, to books I would buy and leave to give with an individual annual birthday note for each of my children until they turned 21.

I packed away the 'Me' folder. I had my future back. Certainty. It had been 50/50. This time it had come out my way. Now the question is:

How will I use this to change my path? Will I use it fully? Will this actually have been the very best week I could have had?

Why am I telling you all this?

STOP, THINK, REVIEW, ASSESS. Don't take the future for granted.

Steve Jobs famously said: *'Remembering that you are going to die is the best way I know to avoid the trap of thinking you have something to lose. Almost everything – all external expectations, all pride, all fear of embarrassment and failure – these things just fall away in the face of death, leaving only what is really important.'*

We know from a relatively early age that we are going to die. We just don't fully believe it will happen to us. As you get older, your mortality becomes more apparent. You start to lead a better life. You understand you have the choice to design your life, understanding the consequences and compromises involved. You can curate the best life for you. There is only one success, writes Christopher Morley: *'To be able to spend your life your own way'.*

Remember the number one regret of people of their deathbeds, as reported by a palliative care nurse: *'I wish I'd had the courage to live a life true to myself, not the life others expected of me'.* In fact, the number one reason why people fail in life is because they listened to their family, friends, neighbours, according to Napoleon Hill. Do not say yes to other people's dreams. As you get older, you never regret the risks you took and failed, but you always regret the risks you did not take.

Ask yourself this – what are the moments you say to yourself: *'This is the real me?'* Are you leading the right life for you?

Never wish for the clock to be turned back. Accept the past as past, without denying or discarding it. Focus on what you can do next. I can't wait till I am 65. How much fun and learning am I going to have in the next 11 years! Let's go!

Here's my final point: **Life is long enough if you use your time and energy well, and maximise it.** Get cracking!

FINAL POSTCRIPT

I have received plenty of feedback over the years that too many *Possums* posts include 'changed my life' in the first sentence. Sorry! I can't find a better descriptor though when I tell you this: writing *Savage Oxygen* HAS changed my life. Here's why.

Big rewards, power, privilege, influence. Just four of the benefits of my role as chief operating officer of a major communications group. So why did I quit, and walk away into a career 'wilderness'? What was the REAL reason I resigned? Okay – here's the truth, and stuff the consequences.

I lived in Adelaide in my early 20s, in a house next to a very senior, 80-year-old Anglican Church minister. He was about to have a major operation, and was nervous about it. I was chatting to him over the fence: '*Oh well, if it goes wrong I guess you'll find out whether what you've been banging on about for 60 years is actually true!*' To his credit, he saw the humour in it, and laughed.

That's why I quit my job. I needed to 'walk the talk'. It was time to take my own medicine. Quite simply, I had to have the courage to take this one critical step. And I did.

I took the 'exit' door when I did not know where the stairs would take me.

Many people die in emergencies because they refuse to take the 'exit' door. They fear the uncertainty of where those stairs lead, and they stay put. With the encouragement of friends and family, I walked through it.

I had been writing and editing this book. The stories reminded me of passionately felt advice I have encouraged readers to take. It was time for me to take my own counsel.

I was unhappy in my role. The learning and passion had slowed. For six years it had been the best role I'd ever had, and a privileged part of my career. I was grateful for the opportunity. But it was time to move on. *'There's no growth in your comfort zone.'* I was cruising. I loved the monthly pay cheque, and the 'pointy end' pace. It was not enough. I had to walk through that exit door.

So I did.

While I don't know exactly where those stairs are going to take me, I do have absolute faith it will be to 'safety'.

I've always been a massive fan of 'making the grass greener on this side of the fence'. Work hard to adjust a role to give it what is missing for you. If that's not possible, don't be a prisoner of cash flow, and fear. Not when you are unhappy. Have courage. Have faith. Of course make sure you plan carefully, and have contingencies in place.

Then – take the 'exit' door. Good things WILL come from it.

ACKNOWLEDGMENTS & THANKS

Thank you to everyone who gave me ideas and inspiration that helped me write these stories – to the colleagues, friends, family, authors, painters, political leaders, journalists and many other sources from which I gathered material. Much of my content is original. Almost all of it is shaped by the thinking of others that I have learnt over the years.

I have tried to acknowledge all those I sourced materials and ideas from in *References & Sources* on the following pages. There is just no way I can remember all of you, or attribute accurately every reference. Please do forgive me if you spot something you said or wrote, and I have not attributed it. Hand on heart, I forgot. If I get something wrong, please forgive me for that too. Send me an email (chris@chrisjohnsavage.com) and I will correct it, or add the attribution to the master copy.

To my brother Greg, thank you for encouraging me to get 'online' and to start my blog five years ago.

To my constant *Possums* partner, Martine L'Eveille: thank YOU for your persistent loyalty, encouragement and love in helping get my weekly posts up and running.

To my former CEO, Mike Connaghan, who supported me from the start to make *Possums* a success. He did not always agree with my views, but was consistent in his support.

To all at Aquent and Firebrand, for being constant supporters and helping build my online brand.

To Stuart O'Brien and his team at Houston, for redesigning the blog website.

To Nick Beckhurst and the team at Brandcraft, for designing the cover and the layout.

To Véronique Bloch in Hydra, for the painting that graces the cover. Visit her store there: The Hydra Trading Company.

To my friend, Simon Burrow, who provided the road map and encouragement from his home in Ménerbes, Provence, to get this book done. To Paula Gaber, my boss and mentor from my Hong Kong days, who generously read the manuscript from her home in the United States.

To Grant Butler and the fine folks at Editor Group, for proofreading and a final once over.

To my nephew Brendon, who did some slave labour to make it all happen.

And to Sally Dowling, who helped on the early drafts of the manuscript, always after hours and above the call of duty, always with humour and enthusiasm.

Finally, to all *Possums* subscribers and followers. Thank you for making me feel relevant. To those reading this now, well done and thank you, for 'showing up'. With appreciation and a very big hug, Chris.

REFERENCES & SOURCES

'The greatest part of a writer's time is spent in reading. In order to write, a man will turn over half a library to make one book.'

Samuel Johnson, quoted in *The Life of Samuel Johnson* by James Boswell, taken by me from *Legacy* by James Kerr.

Books

Albom, M., Tuesdays with Morrie (Doubleday, 1997)

Blair, Tony, A Journey (Random House, 2010)

Boo, Katherine, Behind the Beautiful Forevers (Scribe, 2012)

Bridges, Michelle, Your Best Body (Penguin, 2013)

Carnegie, Dale, How to Win Friends and Influence People (Vermilion, 1998)

Conrad, Barnaby, Fun While It Lasted (Random House, 1969)

Cottrell, D., and Nix, R., Indispensable (McGraw Hill, 2013)

Covey, Stephen R., The 7 Habits of Highly Effective People (Simon & Schuster, 2004)

George, Bill, True North: Discover Your Authentic Leadership (Jossey Bass, 2007)

Glendinning, V., Raffles and the Golden Opportunity (Profile Books, 2012)

Hill, Napoleon and Ritt, Michael, Napoleon Hill's Keys to Positive Thinking (Dulton, 1998)

Huffington, Arianna, Thrive (Harmony, 2014)

Kennedy, Edward, True Compass, A Memoir (Twelve, 2009)

Kerr, J., Legacy: 15 Lessons in Leadership (Constable & Robinson Ltd, 2013)

Klein, D., Travels with Epicurus (Text, 2012)

Landsberger, H., Hawthorne Revisited (Ithaca, 1958)

Lombardi Jr, Vince, The Lombardi Rules (McGraw-Hill, 2003)

Mango, A., Atatürk (Hachette UK, 2011)

Marsh, Nigel, Fit, Fifty and Fired Up (Allen & Unwin, 2012)

McCaw, Richie with McGee, Greg, The Real McCaw (Hachette NZ, 2012)

Morris, Tom, True Success (Berkley Books, 1995)

Newport, Cal, So Good They Can't Ignore You (Hachette, 2012)

Niven, David, The Moon's a Balloon (Penguin UK, 2005)

Parthasarathy, A., The Fall of the Human Intellect (Parthasarathy, 2007)

Peters, Tom, The Brand You 50 (Knopf, 1999)

Peters, Tom, Thriving on Chaos (Harper Business, 1989)

Pink, Daniel L., Drive: The Surprising Truth About What Motivates Us (Canongate, 2011)

Robinson, Sir Ken, The Element (Penguin, 2009)

Seligman, Dr Martin, Learned Optimism (William Heinemann, 2011)

Shakespeare, William, Twelfth Night (Simon & Schuster, 2004: first published 1601)

Soccer, T., Sir Alex Ferguson: The Boss of Old Trafford (Tabloid Soccer, 2008)
Tolle, Eckhart, A New Earth (Plume, 2005)
Tracy, Brian, Earn What You're Really Worth (Vanguard Press, 2012)
Tracy, Brian, Eat That Frog (Berrett-Koehler, 2007)
Waugh, Evelyn, The Sword of Honour Trilogy (D. Campbell, 1994)

Songs
Cohen, L., Going Home (Old Ideas, 2012)
Cohen, L., Anthem (The Future, 1992)
Cohen, L., In My Secret Life (Ten New Songs, 2001)
Dylan, B., The Times They Are A-Changin' (The Times They Are A-Changin', 1964)
Meat Loaf, Two Out of Three Ain't Bad (Bat Out of Hell, 1977)
Midnight Oil, Power and the Passion (10,9,8,7,6,5,4,3,2,1, 1982)
Rodriguez, S., I Wonder (Cold Fact, 1970)

Movies and videos
Citizen Kane (Mercury Productions, 1941)
The Grand Budapest Hotel (Fox Searchlight Pictures, 2014)
The Iron Lady (20th Century Fox, 2011)
Night Train to Lisbon (Lusomundo, 2013)
New Year's Eve (Warner Bros. Pictures, 2011)
Papadopoulous & Sons (Double M Films, 2012)
Perez Hilton interview with Lady Gaga
Searching for Sugar Man (Red Box Films, 2012)
The Best Exotic Marigold Hotel (Fox Searchlight Pictures, 2011)
Tom Peters Leadership Thoughts: Listening (2009)
The Lorax (Universal, 2012)
Zulu (Paramount, 1964)

Additional published sources
Brain Pickings
Collective Magazine
New York Review of Books
TED (www.ted.com)
The International New York Times
The New York Times
The Sydney Morning Herald

Individual sources/quotes/specific attributions (not listed in the 'Books' section)

Woody Allen, Isabel Allende, Catherine Armitage, Mickey Arthur, Mustafa Atatürk, Marcus Aurelius, Sven Baker, Stuart Barnes, Wayne Bennett, Sir Geoff Boycott, Michelle Bridges, Brené Brown, Robbie Brozin, Buddha, Jeremy Bullmore, Phil Burgess, Harold Burson, David Morrison, Dale Carnegie, Captain Richard Champion de Crespigny, Stéphane Charbonnier, Roger Camplisson, Winston Churchill, Paul Cocks, Lee Colan, Mike Connaghan, Calvin Coolidge, Peter Cullinane, Mario Cuomo, Charles Darwin, Neil Davis, Robbie Deans, Edward de Bono, Michel de Montaigne, Andrew Denton, Leonardo da Vinci, Walt Disney, John Eales, Dwight Eisenhower, Edward Eyre, Sir Alex Ferguson, David Fox ('Foxy'), Lady Gaga, Gandhi, John Gardner (of MAGNUS fame), John Gardner (of Stanford Alumni Association fame), Paul Gibson, André Gide, Francoise Gilot, Malcolm Gladwell (Cannes Creativity Festival, 2011), David Gonski, Christopher Graves, Wayne Gretzky, Andy Grove, Toad of Toad Hall, Tim Hamilton Russell, Debbie Harry, Matthew Hayden, Trevor Hendy, Rose Herceg, Margaret Hetterman, Jennifer Horrigan, Mike Howorth, Arianna Huffington, Elbert Hubbard, John Hurst, Rob Irving, Steve Jobs, David Johnson, Paul Keating, Kennedy family, Henry Kissinger, Andy Lark, Geoff Levy, Patrick Looram, Rohan Lund, Steve Lyons, Steve Martin, Bill Marsteller, Groucho Marx, Bruce Matchett, Richie McCaw, Pascal Mercier, Thomas Merton, Christopher Morley, Chris Mort, Tom Moult, Napoleon, John Nicholl, Stuart O'Brien, David Ogilvy, Andrew Parker, General George S. Patton, Jonathan Pease, Pericles, Tom Peters, Edward Phelps, Philo, Picasso, Ange Postecoglou, Creel Price, Sir (Thomas) Stamford Raffles, Cecil Rhodes, Anthony Robbins, Sir Ken Robinson, Eleanor Roosevelt, Theodore Roosevelt, Peter Salt, Vidal Sassoon, Eric Schmidt, Albert Schweitzer, Dr Martin Seligman, Robin Sharma, Bobby Simpson, Simon Sinek, Zadie Smith, Doug Smollan, Socrates, John Steel, John Studdert, Russell Tate, Mother Teresa, Chris Thomson, Thoreau, Brad Thorn, David Tudehope, Mark Twain, Mike Tyson, Mike Walsh, George Washington, Phil Waugh, Jack Welch, will.i.am, Peter Williams, Miles Young, Sun Tzu.

Other sources of inspiration, ideas, content

Andrew Antoniou, Lukas Aviani, Margaret Bennett, Ekkehard Betsch, Fleur Bonnen, Alan Bowman, Mike Boyd, Simon Burrow, Alex Campbell, Paul Carozza, Anouk Darling, Sophie Duffy, John DuVernet, Paula Gaber, John Grooms, Cameron Hall, Alan Higgins, Michelle Hutton, Tom Jaffney, Chris Kelliher, Peter Kingsbury, Neil Lawrence, Harold Mitchell, Rob Martin Murphy, John Mutton, Russell Nash, Matthew Percival, Gary Perlstein, Chris Phyland, Clare Robinson, Grant Rosewarne, Peter Satori, Richard Sauerman, Greg Savage, Ron Savage, David Sawicki, Peter Sekuless, Kamal Sharma, Paul Spon-Smith, Phil Smith, Andrew Stenning, Des Surleff, Peter Sutherland, Tim Sutton, Oscar Trimboli, Justus Veeneklass, Russ Vine, Dudley White, Ian Williams. Note: The jerk who let me down so badly, who lied and deceived? He gets no mention.

And not forgetting ...

A rabbi, Facebook, a bus ticket, a fortune cookie courtesy of the Peacock Gardens, a gym poster in Brisbane, a local fitness trainer, a JWT handbook, Maxus Singapore, Starbucks, a magazine in a Singapore hotel room, New York agency Taxi, Cannes Creativity Festivals (2010, 2011, 2014), Calvin Klein, a grandparent of a relative of John Studdert, someone on their deathbed, Buddhists, a Qantas flight attendant, a Johnnie Walker advert in China, a palliative care nursing sister, a miserable investment banker, Smith Magazine, a University of Sydney graduation ceremony, a truffle farmer from the Luberon, a throat cancer surgeon, and various family members I am not allowed to mention.

Printed in Great Britain
by Amazon